QUICK REFERENCE GUIDE FOR BAND DIRECTORS WHO TEACH JAZZ

QUICK REFERENCE GUIDE FOR BAND DIRECTORS WHO TEACH JAZZ

Ronald E. Kearns

Published in cooperation with the
National Association for Music Education

Rowman & Littlefield
Lanham • Boulder • New York • London

Published by Rowman & Littlefield
An imprint of The Rowman & Littlefield Publishing Group, Inc.
4501 Forbes Boulevard, Suite 200, Lanham, Maryland 20706
www.rowman.com

86-90 Paul Street, London EC2A 4NE

Copyright © 2024 by The Rowman & Littlefield Publishing Group, Inc.

All rights reserved. No part of this book may be reproduced in any form or by any electronic or mechanical means, including information storage and retrieval systems, without written permission from the publisher, except by a reviewer who may quote passages in a review.

British Library Cataloguing in Publication Information available

Library of Congress Cataloging-in-Publication Data

Names: Kearns, Ronald E., 1952– author. | National Association of Music Educators.
Title: Quick reference guide for band directors who teach jazz / Ronald E. Kearns.
Description: Lanham : Rowman & Littlefield Publishers, 2024. | "Published in cooperation with the National Association for Music Education." | Includes bibliographical references and index.
Identifiers: LCCN 2024025552 (print) | LCCN 2024025553 (ebook) | ISBN 9798881801595 (cloth) | ISBN 9798881801601 (paperback) | ISBN 9798881801618 (epub)
Subjects: LCSH: Jazz—Instruction and study—Handbooks, manuals, etc. | Band directors—Handbooks, manuals, etc.
Classification: LCC MT10.K28 Q46 2024 (print) | LCC MT10.K28 (ebook) | DDC 781.65071—dc23/eng/20240611
LC record available at https://lccn.loc.gov/2024025552
LC ebook record available at https://lccn.loc.gov/2024025553

Contents

Acknowledgments	xi
Purpose	xiii
Introduction	1
1 Getting Started: First Steps	**3**
Developing Your Personal Philosophy of Music Education	3
Creating a Support Network	4
Program Description	5
A Sample Jazz Ensemble Handbook	5
Table of Contents	5
Mission Statement	5
General Handbook Description	6
Calendar of Events	6
Concert Attire	6
Fees	6
Festival/Assessment Information	7
Fundraising Overview	7
Grading Policy	7
Developing a Five-Year Plan	8
Recruiting	8

2	**Developing a Jazz Ensemble as Part of Your Band Program**	**11**
	Program Development	11
	Teaching Improvisation	12
	Selecting Students for Jazz Ensembles	14
3	**Things You Need to Do before the First Rehearsal**	**19**
	Organize and Plan	19
	Rhythm Section	22
	Bass	22
	Drum Set	24
	Guitar	25
	Piano	25
	Saxophone Section	26
	Lead Alto Sax	26
	Lead Tenor Sax/Jazz Tenor	27
	Baritone Sax	27
	Trumpet Section	28
	Lead Trumpet	28
	Trombone Section	29
	Lead Trombone	29
4	**Organizing the First Rehearsal**	**31**
	Organizing the First Rehearsal and Classroom Management	32
	Ending the First Rehearsal	34
	Sample First Rehearsal	34
	Warmup	34
	First Rehearsal Song	35
	Sample Lesson Plan	36
	Objective	36
	Warmup	36
	First Rehearsal Piece	37
	Second Rehearsal Piece	37
	Third Rehearsal Piece	37
	End of Rehearsal	38

Contents / vii

5	**Developing Improvisational Skills**	**39**
	Expanding the Palette	40
	Transcribing Jazz Solos	42
	Developing and Using the Jazz Language	42
	Baby Steps	44
	Creating Melodic Lines	45
	Beyond Baby Steps	46
	Learning to Overcome the Fear of Failure	47
	Performance Time	47
6	**Planning Your First Performance**	**49**
	Writing Lesson Plans for Jazz Class	50
	The Performance	51
7	**Festival Preparation and Performance**	**55**
	Festival Information and Description	55
	Preparing to Be Adjudicated	56
	Score Study	56
	Making Notes on the Score	57
	Teaching the Music for Adjudication	57
	Record Your Rehearsals	61
8	**Developing a Jazz Budget Separate from the Band Budget**	**63**
	Travel Expenses	66
	Electronic Equipment	67
9	**Program Maintenance**	**69**
	Developing a Five-Year Plan	69
	Purchasing and Maintaining Equipment	70
	The Importance of Individual Recognition and Praise	71
10	**Using Technology in the Jazz Classroom**	**75**
	Recording Your Group	75
	Using Tablets and Smartphones	77
	Music on a Tablet	78
	Interactive Software	78

	Play-Along Recordings	79
	Websites	79
	Social Media	80
	Facebook	80
	X (Formerly Twitter)	80
	Google	81
	Notation Software	81
	Choosing the Best Notation Software for Your Program	81
	Using Play-Along Software and Hardware	82
	PowerPoint	83
	Videotaping Your Jazz Ensemble	84
	Technology Resources on the Internet	84
	Technology Resources in Book Form	85
11	**Choosing Literature for Your Jazz Ensemble**	**87**
	Suggested Publishers for Jazz Ensemble	87
	Suggested Composers for Jazz Ensemble	88
	Suggested Arrangers for Jazz Ensemble	89
12	**Quick Repairs and Instrument Maintenance**	**91**
	Quick Repairs	91
	Saxophones	92
	Pad Falls Out	92
	Bent Octave Key	93
	Ligature Breaks or Is Missing	94
	Springs Become Unset	95
	Trumpets	95
	Trombones	97
	Amplifiers	97
	Guitar and Electric Bass	98
	Double Bass	98

13	**Developing a Support Group for Your Jazz Ensemble**	**101**
	Establishing a New Parent Group	101
	Leadership Function	103
	Forming Committees	105
	Social Media	106
14	**Trips and Festivals**	**107**
	How Do You Decide What Festivals and Assessments to Participate In?	108
	Trip Logistics	109
	Festival Performance Etiquette	110
	Trip Planning Checklist	111
	International Festivals and Trips	111
15	**Recording Your Group during Rehearsals**	**115**
	Student-Directed Warmups	116
	Microphone Setup and Placement	116
	Common Setups for Microphones	117

Appendix	**121**
Glossary	**123**
Index	**137**
About the Author	**143**

Acknowledgments

When you see a turtle on a fence post, you know it didn't get there by itself. The same is true about writing this book. I could not have written this book without the help of my friends, colleagues, students, and my daughter, Tiffany K. Walker, who is a middle-school band director/teacher.

For thirty years I taught instrumental music in Maryland public schools. Twenty-eight of those thirty years, I taught high school jazz ensembles. During those years I was fortunate to receive help from the late Drs. Thomas DeLaine and Reppard Stone and Dr. Charles "Bud" Caputo. Their guidance helped me find myself as a young director and produce award-winning groups.

After many years of observing me work with bands, my daughter Tiffany K. Walker became a band director. As a band director she has developed outstanding groups and become an outstanding jazz band director. She shared many of her techniques and current trends in jazz education with me for this book.

Most importantly, my students from Forest Park High School, Frederick Douglass High School, John F. Kennedy High School, and Walter Johnson High School helped me hone my skills and develop into an outstanding jazz ensemble teacher/director. None of their groups came in lower than third place in any local, state, national, or international jazz competition. Because those students were willing to follow my instruction, I was able to confidently include my teaching techniques in this book.

Purpose

The purpose of this book is to help classically trained band directors teach and develop jazz programs in their middle school or high school. Unfortunately, most colleges and universities only provide a cursory look at teaching jazz or developing a jazz program. Because of this, most band directors are woefully unprepared to teach jazz. In order to develop a jazz program in your school, you don't have to be a trained jazz musician; you just need a working knowledge of jazz.

This book is written and designed for the purpose of helping you design, develop, and teach jazz in your school. Included in this book you'll find first steps that need to be taken, sample lesson plans, suggested literature, suggested budget development, recruiting, retaining, classroom management, and other basic information for the development of a successful jazz program. Jazz classes require the same discipline and organization as any other instrumental class. One of the biggest mistakes some teachers make is to treat jazz as a lesser music form than classical music. This incorrect assumption means that jazz is not taught with the same demands for precision that classical music is. To develop a good jazz program, band teachers must learn jazz theory and the concepts of jazz. Being a jazz learner before becoming a jazz teacher will help teachers become empathetic with their students and the challenges they will face. Jazz requires an understanding of improvisation and the knowledge base that jazz performers must have.

The mistake a lot of directors make that dooms their jazz groups is to feel as though jazz classes don't require lesson plans or classroom management as concert band classes do. In some ways, jazz classes need more structure than classical classes. Jazz can seem less organized based on its free-spirited style, but the seemingly chaotic nature of jazz performance requires as much if not more structure. Jazz allows students to be innovative within a clear structure, and the teacher must set the parameters in which the "chaos" can exist. Improvisers have to be aware of form and structure in the music being performed that classical players are not required to actively detect. Classical music by nature is clearly written out, and all players know their responsibilities. In jazz, each player must see their part well defined within the group. Improvisation is the act of spontaneously composing *over* a set of jazz chords or chord progressions.

Introduction

This book is designed to be a quick reference guide for the reader. It can be read chapter by chapter, or the reader can go to a specific chapter to get needed information and guidance. Because of this, some chapters have information discussed in previous chapters that reinforce what was written prior or give the reader needed information for specific topics.

The book draws from the author's twenty-eight years of teaching jazz on the high-school level and the contributions of a middle-school jazz band teacher. Teachers who are classically trained and who have never been in a jazz ensemble are the target audience, but teachers who have jazz experience will also find it useful. Unfortunately, a lot of colleges and universities don't include jazz instruction in their methods classes, and future teachers are not always prepared for developing a jazz program in their schools. The book is a step-by-step guide for developing a jazz ensemble from "scratch" or improving an established program.

Teachers using this book are urged to immerse themselves in learning jazz as if they are learning a foreign language. The adage that there are twelve notes in music applies to this approach. Band teachers have a proficiency in reading classical music but are generally not familiar with jazz inflections or concepts. This book addresses ways for teachers to gain a comfort level for teaching jazz concepts.

As you go through the book, you are encouraged to share your challenges learning jazz with your students. Once your students see that you understand the challenges they are encountering, they will follow your advice on how to develop their skills as a jazz performer. Fear is the biggest reason students don't do well learning jazz, but when they discover their fear is normal, it will no longer block the learning process. Believe it or not, your students will respect you more once they see that you are encountering the same challenges they are, but your experience as a trained musician will help guide them through the challenges.

Good luck navigating your way through this process, and use this guide as a GPS on the road to jazz instruction.

1
Getting Started
First Steps

Developing Your Personal Philosophy of Music Education

Having a good personal philosophy of music education is very important. What do you want to impart on your students? How do you see yourself implementing your goals? How do you see music as a tool for student development? How do you view your mission as a music educator? Not every child will become a professional musician, but that doesn't mean they can't have a lifelong involvement with music. Students may become educated audience members, music patrons, or members of amateur jazz groups, but your mission is the same: help them develop a strong appreciation for jazz. Some of your students may become administrators or decision-makers who will decide the fate of music in our schools. Here are some points that you need to include in your personal philosophy:

- Explain how you see music as a lifelong pursuit. Every student won't become a professional musician, but they will become consumers.
- Share how music shaped your development. Include how you see music as an important part of the American educational system.

- Have a complete definition and description of music education in specific terms, avoid generalizing.
- State how jazz allows students to express themselves creatively.

Once you have a clear, concise philosophy formulated you're ready to share it with others. This means creating a support network that will help you get the needed resources to build a strong program.

Creating a Support Network

You can't build a strong jazz program in your school alone. You'll need to get all shareholders to buy into your vision (students, parents, administrators, community members, and school staff). In order to do that, you must be very clear on what you want your program to develop into. Once again, be very specific and avoid meaningless statements that look good on paper.

After you've answered the questions mentioned earlier in your mind, you'll need to write your answers in a succinct statement. That statement should easily explain what you see as your personal mission. If you have a philosophy that speaks only to band, you'll need to tweak it to include jazz. Your personal philosophy of music education will be your contribution to developing a mission statement for each of your performing groups. Your syllabi and lesson plans will reflect the missions of your groups. You will need to create a resource network to help you implement your mission. The National Association for Music Education has *National Standards for Music Education* that list what music education should do. Go to https://www.nafme.org to view these standards. Use these standards to help you shape your personal philosophy, lesson plans, and the overall view of your program.

Program Description

The program description should be stated clearly and unambiguously to make it clear what your program will be. Your vision of the program and what you expect your program to become under your leadership should be stated plainly. It is helpful to allow your students and parents space to help develop or amend the group's mission statement. This helps all stakeholders buy into the goals and mission of the program. Instead of students and parents thinking of jazz ensemble as "your" program, their helping develop the mission statement helps make it "our" program. Ownership of the program will lead to their having accountability in the success or failure of the program based on a mutual vision. The program description is as important as the mission statement.

A Sample Jazz Ensemble Handbook

The following is a sample handbook for jazz ensemble that can be adapted for your use. You should customize it to meet your needs.

Table of Contents

This is where you provide quick reference information for users. You should list all of the contents of the handbook including special dates, expectations, classroom procedures, and so forth.

Mission Statement

This should be a succinct statement of what the jazz program in your school will be. You want to make it clear that the program will meet the needs of all students, will reflect the diversity of the community, and will serve the needs of all students irrespective of race, socioeconomic status, cultural differences, disability, and gender identities. Students, parents, and you should have input into this statement.

General Handbook Description

This is where you include all of the information mentioned previously. It should also include a brief welcome statement for new students and a statement of the importance of having returning students.

Calendar of Events

In this section you should include all the calendar dates that are required for grades and/or awards. Concert dates, assessment dates, trip dates, and any other required performances should be listed. You should also include which dates have mandatory participation and which can be excused without penalization (grade or awards points).

Concert Attire

A simple act that unifies a group is having everyone dressed in a uniform fashion. The handbook should outline the dress requirements and any costs involved. If the school is going to provide the attire, you need to outline the students' requirements for cleaning, maintenance, and repair or replacement costs. If the students are to purchase the attire, you should include the vendor information and purchase costs. You should also state your expectations of appearance for performances (clean and well-kept attire). The important thing to remember is that uniformity in dress can lead to a mindset that in turn leads to the achievement of a unified/common goal.

Fees

If there are fees that must be paid out of pocket, they should be explained in this section of the handbook. You should provide a schedule of when fees are due. It is very important that you itemize what the fees are for. If fundraising will be used to defray trip costs, a breakdown of percentages should be included.

Festival/Assessment Information

Most state music associations have a handbook that has a description of the importance of festival participation and a description of festival grades (I–V). These descriptions should be included in your handbook so that students and parents understand the purpose and importance of festival/assessment participation. Most local, district, and state festivals are not competitions. Groups are graded based on standardized criteria. This provides you with a way of evaluating your jazz ensemble's progress.

You may also wish to include your personal view of festival participation so that students and parents can understand why it's such an important part of your grading policy and why your students are required to participate.

Fundraising Overview

If fundraising will be used to defray students' out-of-pocket expenses, explain that clearly in this section. If you know the schedule of your fundraising activities, include those dates in the calendar section of the handbook. You should be sure to check your school's and school district's policies on fundraising before deciding on fundraisers or fundraiser dates. If the number and kinds of fundraisers will be determined by you and a committee of parents, explain how that process will work.

The National Association for Music Education has helpful information about forming and managing a boosters' group. Go to their website for information you wish to include about boosters.

Grading Policy

Your grading policy should be clearly stated. That includes the percentage of the grade each activity will receive. Class participation, festival participation, tests and assessments, concert and performance participation, special class projects, and other activities are a few of the items that should be included.

Developing a Five-Year Plan

Your five-year plan will be the end product of everything being discussed here. In order for your program to survive for five years or more, you'll need help from the school district, your school administration, the school community, parents, current and former students, and the school faculty and staff. During the first few weeks of school, you should meet with each group separately to explain what you hope to achieve. Explain to them how you see them aiding the program and what you see as the best way for them to support the program. Most schools have a back-to-school meeting with parents in the first few weeks of school. This is your opportunity to meet with parents and give them an opportunity to help your program. Have a list of committees needed: trip chaperones, wardrobe consultants, fundraiser organizers, public relations, social activities, festival and performance helpers, and so on. List all the things that will release you to devote your time to teaching jazz and building a program. Have a sign-up sheet there so that you can have a follow-up meeting to create a jazz boosters group. More on this will be covered later in the book.

Meet with your principal and/or school business manager to find out the amount of funding you have available to develop a budget for music, supplies, and equipment. You'll need to provide school instruments for some students (a drum set, amps, and string basses especially). There are also funds available from some school districts to support jazz programs in schools. Talk to your music supervisor to find out what instruments the district provides for each school and the maintenance budget that's available for each school. Jazz band instruments generally cost more to maintain than most other band instruments.

Recruiting

In order to attract and maintain students, you will need the help of current students and former students (if there had been a jazz program in your school prior to your being there). Personal experience and recommendations from students will carry more weight than any other recruiting/maintaining campaign you may create. In the case that you need to reclaim students, positive one-on-one contact and testimonials will help immensely. Unlike other classes, students can choose electives, and they have a choice whether or not to stay. Knowing that you value their participation goes a long way to keeping them and reclaiming them should they leave. If jazz is not offered as a separate class, you'll need to decide when your jazz group or groups will meet. Some groups rehearse before school, after school, or evenings. Jazz bands like other instrumental classes are cocurricular, so you may have a combination of students who are participating for class credit and those who are participating because they want to play in jazz groups. You will need to explain in your handbook how participants who are not taking the class for credit will be held to the same standards as those taking the class for credit. Awards points and eligibility for a band trip are two ways of holding noncredit students accountable.

Essentials needed to be included in the handbook are performance attire, participation expectations, projected costs for participation, where and how to purchase instruments and equipment, audition and seating requirements, and outside-of-school travel.

2

Developing a Jazz Ensemble as Part of Your Band Program

Program Development

It is difficult to believe that there was a time when jazz ensembles were not considered a part of most schools' band programs. In fact, they had to be justified as having value as part of the total program. Jazz instruction as a class in schools is still not as prevalent as other classical band classes. This means that as a music teacher/band director, you will need to incorporate jazz instruction into your overall program objective and possibly offer the class as a before-school or after-school activity. Some school districts allow before-school and after-school rehearsals to be "for credit" classes (rather than an extracurricular activity). More often, jazz groups are cocurricular.

Stating that your program's goal is to develop each student to their optimum level of performance opens the door for you having different kinds of groups to meet each student's need to express themselves musically. Jazz, by nature, is a constantly challenging musical endeavor. Improvisation, which is a key to jazz performance, is spontaneous composition. This means that as performers, students need to understand chord progressions and how to create musical lines above the progressions. This is what composers expect jazz players to be able to do, and it has to be done instantly and usually in front of an audience (even if that audience is classmates doing their classwork during class). Not all students will be interested in expressing themselves and exposing their weaknesses by improvising, but there is great value in providing them with the tools to try. Fear is the biggest hindrance for young improvisers.

Teaching Improvisation

A lot of band directors are reluctant to teach jazz because they feel inadequate or unprepared. This should not keep you from providing this class for your students. In fact, it will help you as a teacher. As you try to perform jazz, you will discover firsthand what your students are experiencing. Because of this, you will be empathetic with your students and have a greater understanding of what they are going through. You'll also be able to offer personal tips to them based on your discovery process; for example, say, "When I tried to play this, I had to listen carefully to what the rhythm section was playing. I discovered that the piano player was providing notes for me to choose from."

Jazz is a class that requires your students to be analytical, use discovery learning (trial and error), and push themselves to their emotional and creative limits. Unlike what happens performing most classical forms, jazz requires students to incorporate their skills through experimentation rather than simply following the music printed on the score before them. When improvising, students are choosing musical vocabulary that allows them to express themselves. Compare this to what a storyteller does; some stories are short and to the point (with few words used), while others are more involved (very descriptive). Some jazz improvisers will tell short stories slowly (with a few notes or phrases) while others may choose to use a lot of notes fast. It is up to the teacher to help students discover how to best tell their "story."

If you want to develop as a jazz improviser, you have to think about it as learning a new language. When you learned to speak, you learned words that were important to your very existence and then you learned words that improved your quality of life. As you matured you moved from simple statements to more sophisticated statements. You used words and statements that had a logical flow together. You didn't jump from monosyllabic words to multisyllabic words. Most of your speech development depended on you listening to others speak. You chose parents, friends, relatives, and mentors as models for your speech. Before you learned to read or write, you learned the language you spoke completely from listening.

Once you got older, you started listening to speakers who represented what you wanted to emulate. There was something about how they spoke that touched you. You decided that you wanted your speech to flow like theirs did. You would even imitate their speech and mannerisms.

If you haven't guessed, the point is that learning to improvise is learning to speak through your instrument. Improvisation is telling a story with your instrument. In order to tell a story, you must know how to speak. You must have a grasp of the language. You are composing your story spontaneously—in front of listeners expecting you to tell them something good! If people frown while you're talking, it means they're not following what you're saying. The same is true when you're playing and the musicians around you are frowning; they're not following what you're saying.

So how do students learn the jazz language besides listening? They start by developing facility on their instrument. Have them do digital exercises, scales, and arpeggios so that when they listen, they can attempt to play what they have heard.

As you have them listen actively (with an instrument in their hands), they want to be able to imitate what they have heard. Have them play along with the improviser and copy their style, listen to their inflections and how they play notes and phrases. The idea is not for young players to become their clones but to have a starting point to learn how to tell their story. Get your students to listen to as many people playing the same song and notice how different they are. As the great tenor saxophonist Dexter Gordon said, "Listen to vocalists sing the lyrics so that you learn proper phrasing and the importance of words to the telling of the song's story."

If your students have difficulty playing some of the phrases they hear, have them go back to method books to improve technique. Method books are not designed to teach improvisation any more than dictionaries are designed to teach you how to write. The important thing is to unlock their mind by not allowing poor technique to inhibit them. Don't let fear of making mistakes cause them not to experiment. Mistakes can be used somewhere because they came from your students' inner ear. Record them so that they can critique themselves. The importance of not trying to correct themselves as they play is so that they will be more fluid in their playing. Fear of failure will inhibit their development as an improviser.

If students really want to grow, listening to themselves critically and listening to others are equally important. Put them in positions playing with others that will help them try new things. Their story is important to others, so encourage them to tell it.

Selecting Students for Jazz Ensembles

Since jazz classes are electives, there will be some students who opt to take jazz band, but chances are there won't be enough for you to get balanced instrumentation. Some of the players you will need in jazz ensemble may not be found in your band program (guitars, acoustic/electric bass, piano/keyboards, and vocalists). This means that you may have to do school-wide recruiting. First, you should contact your current students and find out if any of them play needed instruments (you'll be surprised by the number of guitarists and pianists there are in most schools). If there are those in your classes who play needed instruments, discuss with them your plans to form a jazz ensemble and what you think their contributions and benefits would be. If there are not, post on your website, bulletin boards in the school, or student news media that you are interested in starting a jazz ensemble and need students who play guitar, bass (acoustic or electric), piano, and drum set (all of your percussionists may not play drum set).

Because jazz ensemble by size will fall below class-size requirements, you may need to convince your administration to waive minimum class-size requirements. One way to do this is to have them average your classes (band classes are usually above maximum class sizes and should balance your class numbers). For example, if class size minimum is thirty students per class and you have twenty students in jazz band and forty students in concert band, have your administration average the number to thirty students per class. This can also be done by taking the total number of students you have each day and dividing that number by the number of classes you teach to get the average of thirty students per class. Do not allow the administration to force you to enroll more students for the jazz ensemble class. Many problems occur because of jazz class overcrowding. Some students will not get a chance to play during class, and discipline problems will occur. It will also be very difficult to reach desired sound balance with unbalanced instrumentation.

Even though most jazz scores call for one player per part, it is possible for you to have two players on rhythm section instruments (guitar, bass, piano, and drums) if you explain to the students that everybody won't be able to play on every song every day. Should you double, it would be wise to make sure each player learns each song. Wind players may need to audition for placement in the class, and that should be addressed in the class description, syllabus and the band handbook. Jazz ensemble instrumentation usually consists of five saxophones (two altos, two tenors, and one baritone) four trombones (sometimes five), five trumpets, one guitar, one bass, one pianist, and one drum set player. Saxophone players are often expected to double on clarinet and/or flute and soprano saxophone.

There should be audition pieces for each instrument furnished to the students beforehand, and students should be told what is expected of them. If possible, furnish the students with a short playing example of the audition material so that they can hear the style required. Doing this will help you determine how well the students will use their "ear" when learning jazz styles and prepare them for using their aural skills while performing.

As mentioned earlier, the mistake a lot of directors make that dooms their jazz groups is to feel as though jazz classes don't require lesson plans or classroom management as concert band classes do.

One of the difficult challenges of jazz band is to get students to be willing to take chances. This means that as the director, you must give students the tools they need to develop their jazz skills. Books that are used for classical music generally shouldn't be used for jazz band, because articulation and expression are different. If you're working with a limited budget and you have to use the same books, you will need to select exercises that you can adapt to jazz performance. If the book uses block chords, rewrite some parts to include major-minor seven chords, known as dominant seventh chords (e.g., C-E-G-B♭), major seventh chords (e.g., C-E-G-B), or minor-minor chords (C-E♭-G-B♭). These chords will help your students develop their aural abilities to hear jazz tonalities. If the book uses major scales, instead of starting on the tonic (first note of the scale), start them on the seventh note and ascend to the seventh note an octave higher and, without repeating the seventh, descend the scale and end on the seventh an octave lower. When using eighth notes, because the stress will be placed on the second half of the beat, students will begin to hear how to swing eighth notes and how they should be played (stress or emphasis on the second eighth note). This will be discussed in more detail later in the book when discussing jazz class lesson plans.

One of the most difficult tasks you will face is getting classical students to hear and comprehend the differences between classical and jazz melodies, harmonies, and rhythmic structures. Because some of the elements of jazz are found in other popular music, you can use your students' love of popular music to teach jazz concepts. This is where having guided listening sessions will help. As you and your students listen, you can point out the differences between how jazz music is approached by jazz players. Twelve-bar (twelve-measure) blues songs are a good starting point. The blues form in twelve bars/measures will have a short motif statement (four bars), slight variation (four bars), and repetition of the original statement. You should select model

Developing a Jazz Ensemble as Part of Your Band Program / 17

big bands such as the Duke Ellington Orchestra, the Count Basie Orchestra, Stan Kenton's big band, and modern bands like Christian McBride's big band. Military big bands such as the Navy Commodores, the Air Force's Airmen of Note, or the Army's Army Blues big band have special educational outreach programs and will come to your school or send you recordings and helpful materials. You can contact them directly or have your local military recruiter contact them for you.

3

Things You Need to Do before the First Rehearsal

Organize and Plan

Having an organized first rehearsal is very important for the establishment of a good jazz program. This includes having the proper equipment, having accessible music for all players, and making sure each student knows how they and their part fit in with the big picture. One of the first and most important things you'll need to do before you have your students play is to have a day of guided listening. In order for them to understand the difference between playing classical music and playing jazz, they must hear the difference. You should go to YouTube or a music-streaming service to find players and groups for your students to model. Jazz articulations and interpretations are very different from classical music, and it's important for students to hear the nuances that make jazz unique. There are two types of listening that jazz players use: active and passive listening. Starting with passive listening, jazz players listen without their instrument. They listen to different styles and musicians to settle in on the style and musicians they like. Once they hear the different styles, they can begin to list groups and individuals they like. They can mentally start to visualize themselves as a performer in the group or playing like a member of the group. Once this phase of passive listening has been completed, serious jazz players move to active jazz listening. Active listening is done with the instrument in hand. During active listening, students should pause the recording and attempt to play what they heard. They need to imitate the articulations and inflections they hear. The first step of active listening is to learn the heads (melodies) of the song they are focusing on. As they play the heads, they should concentrate on jazz inflections and other nuances. This is the essence of learning the jazz language. Improvisation is basically playing variations on a theme. Before you can create a logical variation, you must first know the theme. Once your students are familiar with the theme, the next step is to learn to play their favorite player's solo, note for note. There are many software programs and devices that allow you to slow down and/or stop the solo to play licks or patterns. Players should pay attention to how the soloist uses riffs, scales, and licks. This is where method books come in. Locate the riff or pattern in a method book and have students learn it in all twelve keys. Once they have transcribed the solo, the next step is to play along with the recording and substitute some of their ideas for the soloist's ideas. The goal is to continue until they have substituted all of their ideas for what the soloist has played. Students should record themselves and compare what they did with the original solo. There's no time limit for learning songs by transcribing. The important thing is for students to learn what the artist is doing and to imitate it until they can freely express their ideas through improvisation. Obviously, this process is not going to happen in one or two rehearsals, so the goal is to introduce it as an ongoing process.

Here are some play-along resources—jazz play-along software—that can be used:

Amazing Slow Downer
Band-in-a-Box
Genius Jamtracks
iReal Pro
JAMMATES
Jazz300

Things You Need to Do before the First Rehearsal / 21

JJazzLab
Real Book
SessionBand
Tomplay

Students can download most of these to their phones and tablets.

One of the most important things a jazz instructor can do to have a successful jazz ensemble or combo is to help students understand the concept of swinging. The first step in this process is to provide audio and video recordings of model groups. The second thing is to help players understand the function of their instrument and their responsibilities as players. YouTube has a wealth of videos of live performances and entire albums to listen to and/or watch. Before you play or suggest them for your students, be sure to screen them first. If you are near an area where there are professional jazz performers, invite them to your school or go out to one of their live performances. If you get to be around these professionals, arrange for your students to ask them about how they view their function in the group. There's nothing like one-on-one contact for your students to learn firsthand. With technology, you can arrange Zoom, Skype, Google Meet, or FaceTime interactions. Whatever you do, make listening the first step. At this point, a description of swing helps. Swing in this case does not refer to the period of music known as the Swing Era, it's a style of playing.

If there is any section that is responsible for swing, it is the rhythm section. Swing in this case refers to the feeling of the emphasis on beats two (2) and four (4) rather than on the strong beats of one (1) and three (3) in common time (4/4). This feeling of syncopation is one of the reasons jazz was often generally referred to as "syncopated music" in the early days of its development.

Each section of your jazz ensemble has a specific function, and that function is based on the timbre of the instruments in that section. You should explain the function and concepts of each section clearly to your students (explain the functions during a listening session so that students have concrete examples to refer to). The only section that is not made up of "like" instruments is the rhythm section. Though the rhythm section is made up of instruments that are totally different, it is the unity of this section that makes the band "swing." Following is a description of each instrument in each section and a brief discussion of the function of each section.

Rhythm Section

One of the best model rhythm sections for large jazz ensembles comes from the Count Basie Orchestra. The players in this great group defined what swing was to be. They include William "Count" Basie (piano), Freddie Green (guitar), Walter Page (bass), and Jo Jones (drums). Each of these players had a style that has been imitated and refined over the years. The Jamey Aebersold series has recordings available that allow each rhythm section instrument to play along with CDs or streaming services that will help them learn their function (Jamey Aebersold Music). One of the supplemental books for the series gives piano voicings that are commonly used in jazz (*Piano Voicings*, from the *Volume 1 Play-A-Long,* Jamey Aebersold Music). The Aebersold jazz voicings can be used for basic blues as well with jazz standards. Dan Haerle also has a book that teaches piano voicings for jazz, rock, and pop piano playing (*Jazz/Rock Voicings for the Contemporary Keyboard Player*, Warner Bros. Publishers). Another book recommended by piano players and jazz educators is *Standardized Chord Symbol Notation* by Clinton Roemer and Carl Brandt. This book has common chord spellings and chord forms used in most music scores. These books are very good for students who have little or no training in playing jazz chord progressions.

Bass

It is the function of the bass to keep the time. One of the problems young jazz groups have is for the drummer to attempt to be the timekeeper. This usually creates a "vertical feel" with accents on one and three. For a jazz group to swing, the strong beats must be on two and four. This gives a linear feel that doesn't start over every time you get to a bar line. Walter Page achieved this by playing lines where the strong notes fell on two and four. Think of playing a major scale starting on the seventh degree. Using quarter notes, if seven is on beat one, leading to eight means the resolution from seven to eight leads you from a weak note (demanding resolution) to a strong note (the resolution). Now all of the accents shift, and two and four are the notes of resolution, or strong beats. You feel constant motion in a horizontal line rather than a vertical line with accents on one and three. This is the foundation of the swing feel, but it can't stand alone.

One of the most important responsibilities of the bass is to keep a steady driving beat. The bass is often referred to as the pulse of the jazz ensemble. It will create melodic lines under the chord progressions that will form the basis for harmonization. Sometimes bass lines are written out, but the most advanced charts allow the bass player to create their own bass lines. This means that the bass player must have a good concept of chord progressions and how chords are spelled out horizontally rather than vertically. Sometimes all the bass player has written out on their part are chord symbols. This is usually done for swing charts (Latin, rock, and fusion generally have parts that are written out). When playing swing charts, the bass player becomes the lead player in the rhythm section. If the tempo of your band is a problem (speeding up or slowing down), the section you should immediately look at to solve the problem is the rhythm section. Most directors walk over and stand in front of the rhythm section and clap or snap their fingers. This alerts the rhythm section of their primary function—keeping steady time. Simply standing in front of the rhythm section brings their attention to the problem and helps them unify around the beat. Audiences generally aren't aware of what's going on unless the conductor starts to conduct or loudly count off.

Drum Set

The function of the drum set is to complement the bass and give emphasis on two and four. Jo Jones did this with the hi-hat (sock cymbal) by clapping the cymbals on two and four. He also used patterns on the ride cymbal to play eighth notes, with emphasis on the second eighth note in a two-eighth-note pattern. Kenny Clarke developed a pattern he and others called "spang-a-lang" because that's how the pattern sounds (two eighth notes followed by a quarter note). One of the first things you should do with young drummers is remove the bass drum pedal. Drummers playing the bass drum on one and three negates all that the bass is doing. The bass drum should be used for kicks and accents that will add emphasis to horn lines that have nothing to do with swinging. Each part of the drum set serves a different purpose. In general, the hi-hat cymbal establishes beats two and four, commonly known as the back beat. The large cymbal known as the ride cymbal is used to add stylistic elements to the music. Each part of the ride cymbal gives a different sound. The closer to the bell of the cymbal the drummer plays (near the top), the less ring the cymbal will have. The farther from the bell the player plays, the more ring the cymbal will have. Drummers need to experiment with stick placement on the cymbal to determine which sound should be used for various styles of music. The pattern known as the swing pattern is played in varied eighth-note patterns on or near the edge of the cymbal. Another large cymbal is known as the crash cymbal. This cymbal is used to add extra emphasis or punctuations to parts of music that are intended to stand out or add a degree of completeness to the music parts that are intended to stand out. As your students listen, they will learn how to use the bell of the crash cymbal played in tandem with the ride cymbal to create different colors. This is especially true when playing rock, Latin, or fusion styles of music. Once the drummer listens to recordings, they learn to use hits on the snare drum for added emphasis and to push the swing feel forward.

Guitar

Freddie Green developed two styles that have defined the function of the guitar in large jazz ensembles. The first style is to play chords on each beat of the measure. Strumming on each beat is much more difficult to do than it sounds. Combined with what the bass and drums are doing, the guitar helps keep the beat steady by playing on each beat. The second thing Freddie Green did was to play a "comping" pattern. Comping got its name by being complementary to what the bass, drums, and soloists are doing. The pattern is based on a dotted quarter note followed by an eighth note. Comping is most often done by the pianist now, in combos or big bands.

Piano

The piano is the main chord-playing instrument for the band and generally doesn't play on the beat. The chords the piano plays will furnish the harmonies and form the basis for improvisers to be able to follow the song's chord progressions. Jazz pianists play the comping pattern more often than any other harmonic instrument. By using the comping pattern, pianists add emphasis to selected places in the music. Piano players, even more than bass players, have to have a thorough understanding of music theory. Most jazz charts only provide a chord sketch. Those sketches do not include piano voicings. It's the responsibility of a player to know how to spell out each chord based on the written progressions. It will be helpful to young players for you to take out time to write out chord choices for them. Jamey Aebersold, Dan Haerle, and Jerry Coker have books that can help you. With a little guidance, you can help them design the rhythms they should use for their comping patterns. Remind them (especially in the early stages) that less is more. This means that since chords are written out for wind parts, it's not necessary for them to play a lot of chords. They should be taught to simply fill in the blanks—provide chords where none is being played by other instruments. You can start younger players off playing one note with the left hand and two notes with the right.

The lowest note can be the chord's root note, and the third and fifth or the third and seventh can be played. The third should be included because it will determine the quality of the chord (major or minor). Once the player becomes comfortable, you can have them play two notes in each hand. The pianist must be careful not to play solos or lines while others are soloing. They must rhythmically vary the chords and comping patterns. If you have a guitarist and a pianist, you should have them play chords in different ways. Should the pianist play a chord using the 1, 3, 7, the guitar should play the 1, 5, 9 or a chord voicing that doesn't have each player using a voicing that causes an unbalanced chord. Have one of the players use first or second inversion while the other uses the chord in root position. The dominant is called that because the fifth note when doubled will dominate the sound.

Saxophone Section

If there is any wind section that colors the band or is used to introduce melodic ideas, it is the saxophone section. When the saxophones are not carrying the melody, they are playing sweeping, moving lines that are countermelodies, complementary lines to the melody. Because of the nature of saxophone instruments' sound, the saxophone section blends with brass instruments to create a more mellow overall sound. If brass instruments are known for providing the punch for a band, saxophones are known for "rounding out" the sound of the band.

Lead Alto Sax

Lead alto is the name given to the first alto saxophone part. The lead alto saxophone's function is similar to the lead trumpet function, but because it does not project in the same way as a trumpet, its purpose is to soften the effects of the brass section ("soften" in this case does not refer to volume, it refers to texture). Because of the design of the instrument, the lead alto plays fast lines of music and leads the saxophone section through soli lines (harmonized solos played by the entire saxophone section at the same time). The lead alto controls the overall color of the band along with the lead trumpet. The lead alto, the lead trumpet, and the lead trombone sit in a line in the middle of the big band setup.

Lead Tenor Sax/Jazz Tenor

The lead tenor is known as the jazz tenor because most big band solos are written for the first tenor saxophone player. In jazz scores for younger bands, solos are usually written out for the first tenor sax player. As you work to develop your band, you can assign solos to the students who are most interested in playing a solo. Even if the solo is written out for the first tenor, you can rewrite it for whatever instrument is willing or able to play a solo.

After explaining the function of each of the individual instruments, the next important discussion will be how sections should work together and how they function within the group. The best description of a jazz ensemble (eighteen-piece big band) is that it is a rhythm section and three wind instruments: trumpet, saxophone, and trombone. The most used big band setup has the lead trumpet, lead trombone, and the lead alto all lined up with the lead alto on the front row, lead trombone on the second row and lead trumpet on the third row (in the center of the band). Some bands have the trumpets standing throughout performances, some have trumpets and trombones standing, and some have each section seated with the trombones and the trumpets on risers (in graduated heights). There are several different kinds of setups for jazz ensemble, but for the purposes of this book we will use the three-row system with the rhythm section stage left of the conductor.

Baritone Sax

The baritone sax is the lowest voice of the saxophone section. The "bari sax" can double the lead alto an octave lower, double the bass trombone, or double the bass to bring out the bottom sound of chords or soli lines. Because intonation is built from the bottom up, it's important that the bari sax projects well. Balance of sound, balance of chords, and the establishment of the ensemble balance are important functions of the baritone saxophone.

Trumpet Section

The range and design of the trumpet make it the instrument that brings "punctuations" and added emphasis to the jazz ensemble. If saxophones add mellowness, trumpets add brashness to the band. It is the careful blending of these two kinds of instruments that gives the jazz band its unique sound. Most big band charts (scores) have sections written in that are punctuated and/or led by the trumpet section, with the lead trumpet playing the highest notes of any instrument. During soli sections (harmonized solos or ensemble solos), the trumpet section leads the band. The trumpet section is also the driving force for tutti sections (full ensemble sections). This is what's known as the "shout section" of a piece. The shout section is the climax of most big band pieces. There can be more than one tutti section in a jazz ensemble chart, and the trumpet section provides the "punch" for each of them.

Lead Trumpet

Lead trumpet is the distinction given the first trumpet part of a jazz score. The lead trumpet is the color instrument of the big band; generally, it plays high notes and punctuates specific parts of the music. In jazz band scores, the lead trumpet has the responsibility to "lead" the band through the "shout." In some advanced high-school scores, lead trumpet parts can go up to D above the staff. This means that the lead trumpet player must be able to not only hit high notes but also play in the upper register comfortably. Generally, in order to play in the upper register comfortably, the player needs to be able to "hit" two or three notes above the desired note. When you select music for your band you need to be familiar with the lead trumpet's range. The lead player's biggest job is to establish the style and interpretation for the trumpet section and the ensemble. The character of the big band is determined by the lead trumpet player.

In most big band charts, the second trumpet player does most of the improvising but any player other than the lead trumpet can solo. Lead trumpet can improvise solos but generally you'll want to save their embouchure (chops) so that they can fulfill their main function. The other voices in the trumpet section fill out the chords either by playing block chords or moving harmonized lines.

Trombone Section

Sometimes overlooked in jazz ensembles, the trombone section has many important functions. Thought of as being "big trumpets," these instruments serve a much more important function. Most arrangers and composers use the trombone section to play block chords or moving chords to reinforce the chord progressions being played by the piano and/or the guitar. Because they are brass instruments, their timbre allows them to "cut through" and bring emphasis to the chord progressions with or without the trumpets. The flexibility of the instrument also allows it to add subtle nuances that other members of the ensemble can't. Since it has a slide rather than keys, it can literally slide from chord to chord giving the music a special effect.

Lead Trombone

Lead trombone is the distinction given the first trombone part. The function of the lead trombone is to play the highest voice parts of the trombone section and to function as the big trumpet complementing the lead trumpet (sometimes playing the same musical lines an octave lower). The lead trombone establishes the articulations and interpretations for the entire trombone section. There are usually four trombones in the trombone section, and depending on the score, there could be five. The lead trombone will be seated directly in front of the lead trumpet and behind the lead alto.

The rest of the trombone section harmonizes the score, playing the inner voices of chords. The bass trombone sometimes doubles the baritone saxophone or the fourth trumpet to bring emphasis to the lower notes of a chord.

4
Organizing the First Rehearsal

Music selection and rehearsal pacing are the two most important facets of the first rehearsal. The success of your first rehearsal will have a lasting impact on your program's growth and success. How your students feel at the end of the rehearsal will affect future rehearsals. Ideally, you want the rehearsal to end with your students eager to come back for the next rehearsal. Pacing is important because you don't want to skirt over problems or spend too much time on a problem, causing your students to be bored. Much care has to be taken to choose literature that will be challenging but not discouraging. In every group there will be students who are motivated and can play well. These students will master the music you choose. Conversely, there will be students who are less motivated and have less skill, who will find it difficult to master the pieces you choose. Finding a "happy medium" between these two dynamics will be your challenge.

One way to challenge advanced players is to transcribe parts that are in the original score that may not be in the arrangement you're doing. You may be able to pair weaker players with advanced players as a team-building exercise. Before pairing the players, make sure personalities and attitudes are compatible.

During the rehearsal you will need to help students maintain their focus. Help them identify the melodic line and use cross-listening skills to maintain proper balance and not drown out the melody. One of the reasons jazz bands use the setup they use is so that lead players are in alignment and can clearly hear one another. What you do in the first rehearsal should be transferable to every piece you will work on all year. Focus on teaching skills, not things that are not going to be used in future performances. This also points out the importance of selecting pieces for the semester or year that reinforce good jazz playing. Plan and choose your musical selections based on what you want to achieve and what you expect your group to become. Whatever successes or problems you have in the first performance will be a direct result of your first rehearsal. Organization and planning will be the keys to your success.

Organizing the First Rehearsal and Classroom Management

Before your first downbeat in your first rehearsal, you should have some things in place. Students should know how much time they have to get their instruments and music and be seated. Once that amount of time has passed, you should be ready to begin your rehearsal. Unlike bands, jazz bands have a guitar and a bass that need to tune. Using a tuner, your guitar and bass can tune quickly (if you're using an acoustic piano, tune to it). Group tuning should be done after individual players have tuned their instruments. Start by tuning A first. That way all players can tune and fine-tune together. The final act should be to tune everyone at the same time. In the first few rehearsals this may be time consuming, but the amount of time shortens with each rehearsal once your students know the regimen. For good saxophone intonation, tune the altos and baritone to Concert D. Have your students download a tuning app to their phone so that they can check their intonation regularly while playing.

Once the group is tuned, your first rehearsal selection should be a warmup. The purpose of this first warmup is to get the group to follow you and listen to one another. Many young jazz bands will be "top heavy," having more top parts than lower

Organizing the First Rehearsal / 33

parts (especially fewer trombones). It's important that you get them to listen from the bottom up for ideal balance.

The rehearsal should be divided into at least three parts—warmup, rehearsal piece, and cooldown. The rehearsal selections after the warmup in the first rehearsal will map out where you're going. These pieces will represent what your first performance will be. How you teach the rehearsal pieces will show students your expectations and what being in your class will entail. This is when and how you will establish your standards and what the character of your jazz band will be.

It's very important when working with the first rehearsal pieces that your students understand the importance of pitch accuracy and intonation. As the conductor you must have a clear understanding of the pieces. You will need to give articulation directions that are consistent with the style and period of the literature. These items affect the sound. Before your students play passages with these articulations, you have to give clear descriptions based on the style or period. Needless to say, you must be familiar with how these articulations are played in each period and each sound. During the rehearsal there are no "little things" that can be fixed later. Everything covered in the first rehearsal is a "big thing." If students think that being "close" is good enough, that's how they will approach future performances of the music. Striving for perfection is how you achieve excellence. You may not achieve perfection (no one does), but you can achieve excellence through performance accuracy.

Something that has happened during and after virtual learning is that instrumentation for jazz ensembles has changed. There are instruments that are normally found in jazz ensembles that are not found there now. This may mean that in the first rehearsal, you may need to transcribe parts to make sure that all of the parts on the score are covered. As was mentioned earlier, you don't want your group to be top heavy. Students who can't play advanced lines can play long tones that form the harmonic structure. This serves two purposes: (1) it fills out the harmonic structure of the piece, and (2) it keeps all of your students engaged.

Ending the First Rehearsal

The way you end the rehearsal is as important as the way you began the rehearsal. There should be a clear description of how you expect students to be prepared for the next rehearsal (practice expectations) and what you will cover in the next rehearsal. The rehearsal should not end with the students not feeling as if something has been accomplished. A statement like "Today was a good start, but there are a few things we need to clean up" will give positive reinforcement but also establish expectations. This leads into what's expected in future rehearsals. It also points out the importance of having a unit plan comprised of daily lesson plans. Each daily lesson plan should take you to your terminal objective—a successful final performance. The lesson should conclude with students having a sense of accomplishment but also an awareness that there is more to be done. You should record the first rehearsal so that you can have a guided listening exercise with your students and they can hear what you hear. Recording the group will also give you an archive of recordings that document your group's growth.

Sample First Rehearsal

Warmup

The warmup for the first rehearsal should be something everyone can play. It's important that in the first rehearsal everyone is playing during the warmup. You want to have your students use cross-listening skills to develop good group intonation, phrasing, and overall interpretation. If the warmup piece is too difficult, students will be too busy concentrating on their parts to listen to others across the band. Teach them the blues scale (C, E♭, F, G♭, G, B♭, C) and the minor pentatonic scale (C, E♭, F, G, B♭, C) as source scales. Next choose a song like Sonny Rollins's "Sonnymoon for Two" as your first warmup tune. "Sonnymoon for Two" is nothing but the minor pentatonic scale written as a jazz melody. The scale is played three times in twelve bars (measures) with embellishments to connect the scales. After you play the "head" (melody), have every student attempt to play an improvised solo. By doing this in the first rehearsal, you set the expectation that everyone will try to solo in your "safe place" and "tell their story" to the rest of the class. This is why you teach them the minor pentatonic and blues scales. Obviously, they won't all be able to play polished solos in the first rehearsal, but they will be taught to take the risks required and to overcome their fear. Remind them that there are no wrong notes and that they are always a half step up or down to a note that will "sound better" above the chord changes.

First Rehearsal Song

The first rehearsal song/tune should be challenging but playable. You want this tune to be a song that can be programmed for your first performance. Remember, how your students feel about this first song will affect how they feel about your class and/or the group. You don't want them to necessarily be able to play through the piece the first time through, but you want them to be able to recognize that with practice and preparation they will be able to master it. Choose a piece that embodies all of the things that you have explained or played for them. They need to be able to recognize the jazz articulations and stylistic approaches that the pieces from your guided listening demonstrated. The same is true for the second and third pieces you introduce. At the conclusion of the rehearsal, assign a section of the piece or pieces that you want them to practice at home or outside of class. Some teachers choose to end the first rehearsal with a fun but meaningful activity that will make their students anxious to come back for more. Say something encouraging that lets them know that though they may not have done as well as they expected, you can see from what they did that they are going to be able to eventually perform the songs well. Never allow them to leave class feeling defeated or that they did not meet your expectations.

Sample Lesson Plan

Lesson plans must be a part of your overall objective, so your lesson plans should be part of your unit plan, which should be the "road map" to a successful performance. Lesson plans and unit plans should be spelled out in measurable behavioral objectives. These objectives should state specific outcomes, and the teacher should constantly reinforce how the plans and objectives relate to the terminal objective. The terminal objective should relate directly to the final performance each semester. Students must have a clear understanding of the importance of following the lesson plans until all objectives have been satisfactorily completed. The constant theme is that "close enough" is not good enough or acceptable.

Objective

During the rehearsal we will focus on cross listening for accurate attacks and releases, intonation, and accurate jazz interpretation. Using the warmup piece and three rehearsal pieces, students will actively listen to one another in order to begin and end phrases together, play in tune with one another, and use stylistic articulations in order to interpret and perform with periodic and stylistic accuracy.

Warmup

Students will perform the blues scale and the minor pentatonic scale to fine-tune their instruments. The class will then apply the minor pentatonic scale to "Sonnymoon for Two" by Sonny Rollins. We will do "Sonnymoon for Two" starting on Concert B♭. The group will learn the song by rote in order to develop their ear for "in-the-moment accuracy" so that they can quickly learn future warmups by using their ears to discriminate correct notes from incorrect notes.

First Rehearsal Piece

After completing the warmup with attention having been given to intonation, attacks and releases, and stylistic interpretations, the group will sight-read "C Jam Blues" by Duke Ellington. This piece demonstrates how using only one note with accurate articulations and phrasing can be interesting and engaging for the listener. Students will be encouraged to attempt to solo on top of the rhythm changes (chord progressions). You as the teacher are encouraged to perform along with the class on their main or secondary instruments. This is important because the students will see how you are being challenged by the class objectives and how you resolve the issues you face. You will also be able to understand and empathize with the students and offer practical advice from your experience.

Second Rehearsal Piece

The second rehearsal piece will be "Li'l Darlin'," by Neal Hefti. This piece is very slow, and attention will be focused on intonation and attacks and releases. Because slow pieces require good airflow for good intonation and enough air to sustain a phrase, students must pay attention to what others are playing so that they may start and end phrases and musical lines together and make sure all phrases match stylistically. Poor intonation is easily heard when notes and chords must be sustained for a long period. The class will not rehearse the entire piece but will play through as much of the piece as possible in order to match the class objectives. Attention will be given to all facets of an accurate performance from the very start, and nothing will be glossed over. The goal is to attempt to achieve 100 percent accuracy even though the reality is that nothing will ever achieve 100 percent perfection.

Third Rehearsal Piece

In order to have a variety of styles for your performance, the third rehearsal piece should be a Latin piece or a jazz/rock piece.

Because Latin and jazz/rock pieces rarely use swing eighth notes, articulations will need to be addressed differently. Legato tonguing is not as prevalent as hard attacks (marcato, tenuto accents, and staccato attacks). Students will be expected to attack these notes accurately and release uniformly. This reinforces the need to do accurate cross listening to match not just within sections but across sections. The comparison of relay runners accurately passing the baton clearly helps students visualize passing phrases from section to section cleanly. Because this is such an important concept, time will be needed to achieve accuracy. Articulation, attacks and releases, phrasing, and stylistic interpretations will be ongoing from rehearsal to rehearsal. This means that there can be no "almost" correct. These elements will be keys to an accurate and proficient performance. Everything done in rehearsal should be done with the finished product in mind.

End of Rehearsal

The lesson should end with a piece that will cause the students to practice outside of class and be anxious to come back to class to work on the pieces for class the next day. During the first rehearsal you won't have a piece for everyone to play through, so a "head chart" like the warmup should be used. This is a cooldown piece; it should be interesting enough for students to want to play it and challenging enough to motivate students to practice. It should also have all of the skill requirements that you've worked on in warmups and preparatory pieces. "Blue Bossa" and other songs from Jamey Aebersold recordings are perfect for cooldown.

5

Developing Improvisational Skills

One of the most difficult challenges a jazz performer faces is learning to improvise over jazz progressions (commonly known as playing the changes). The best way for a classically trained teacher to learn how to teach improvisation is for the teacher to attempt to improvise. As you attempt to improvise, you discover the challenges your students will face. Because you are a trained musician, you will be able to adjust to the challenges more quickly than your students. As your students observe you utilizing your listening skills and chord/scale knowledge in order to put together a coherent solo, they will recognize the challenges involved and become interested in problem-solving and using the same skills. You will be able to share with them the challenges you faced as you were struggling to find the "right notes" to play. You will also be able to address "being in the moment" as you listen to the rhythm section and communicate with them in the same way jazz musicians do onstage.

The reason the warmup is so important during the first rehearsal is that you focused on two scales that are important for improvising. Without knowledge of the other scales or jazz clichés, students can craft an engaging solo just from the blues scale and minor pentatonic scale. Because the warmup focuses on using the ear to find "the right note," students should not be intimidated by having no printed music in front of them. The biggest adjustment classically trained musicians face is having no music in front of them while improvising and having to "spontaneously compose" while others are listening. Overcoming fear is the biggest challenge to most improvisers (there will almost always be one player who is a natural improviser).

Most successful jazz teachers are good nurturers. They find ways to encourage their students and correct them without putting out the fire in them. Rather than telling the students they played the wrong notes, nurturing directors say something like "That was good but if you play a G over the C chord, it will probably sound better. Try it and see." The student doesn't feel bad about experimenting, and you don't stifle their creativity. They will want to solve the problem and therefore want to keep trying until they like their note choices.

Expanding the Palette

Using the blues scale and the minor pentatonic scale is a good starting point but won't be enough to sustain a quality solo. After playing one chorus, improvisers will find themselves repeating notes or patterns. To provide students with an expanded palette means introducing more scales for more note choices. This is when you add modes and different scale forms. Yusef Lateef and Walt Weiskopf have books filled with jazz patterns that are based on different modes, but before you introduce their books, you should teach the modes (Walt Weiskopf has books that include a bank of scales and patterns).

There are seven modes that are built from scales that start from each degree of the major scale. The scale starting on the first degree is known as the Ionian. The second degree is the Dorian mode, third degree is the Phrygian, fourth is the Lydian, fifth is the Mixolydian, sixth is the Aeolian, and the seventh is the Locrian. Each mode starts on the stated degree of the scale and goes up an octave using the key signature of the host scale (e.g., in the key of C the Dorian mode will be D, E, F, G, A, B, C, D—all naturals like the C Major scale). Three of the most used modes are the Ionian (I chord), the Dorian (ii chord) and the

Mixolydian (V chord). Students can play the modes as a scale or extract the notes 1, 3, 5, 7 from the mode being indicated by the chord progressions. The ii, V, I progression is known as the "turnaround," and, as the name implies, it is used to turn the improviser around to start the next chorus.

During the warmup, have your students experiment with the modes, using their ears to determine what sounds right to them. Remember, there are no "wrong notes," just right notes that should be used in a different place. This wording helps prevent you from stifling novice improvisers. Using the term "wrong" inhibits them. They become preoccupied with trying not to make mistakes rather than crafting a good solo that is fluid. Once again, improvisation is spontaneous composition while others are listening. Improvisers can't erase notes like paper composers can. You don't get a "do over" during a live performance.

There are many ways students can work on improvisation outside of class. The most used methods are the *Play-A-Long* recordings by Jamey Aebersold. These recordings provide students with play-along tracks for the most played jazz standards and original songs by some of the top jazz performers of all time. You can also use the songs from the recordings for your warmup. If you use the songs on the recordings, you can assign your students homework that you can grade them on (Smart-Music enables you to have your students submit their best work to you via email). There are lots of apps and computer software that can be used as play-alongs that allow the student to speed up or slow down the tempo without affecting the pitch.

Every student, including your bassists and percussionists, should be required to improvise. Obviously, percussionists on drum kit will not be playing modes, but they still need knowledge of what pitched instruments are playing. Have them play on a mallet instrument so that they can learn the importance of being a linear player rather than playing vertically (linear means playing rhythms melodically using drums and cymbals to play lines). Drummers need to know melodies and forms just as pitched instrument players do.

Transcribing Jazz Solos

One of the best ways to learn improvisation is to analyze what jazz improvisers are playing. This process is known as transcribing. There are two ways to transcribe. One way is to listen to recordings and play along, playing what the soloist is playing note for note. This helps the student develop their ear and recognize patterns, chords in arpeggio form, and scales/modes the soloist is using. The second way requires more advanced music knowledge. It involves attempting to write out the solos note for note. The student must be able to write rhythms, chords, and melodic patterns. There are many books available that have transcribed solos by John Coltrane, Charlie Parker, Cannonball Adderley, and others. Seeing those written solos will help students recognize jazz notation. This brings us to the need for passive listening and active listening. Passive listening is done without the instrument. The student listens carefully to each note, phrase, and line. That process leads to active listening. Active listening is done with the instrument in their hands and pausing the recording to play a "lick." Once the student is satisfied with how they play a particular lick or phrase, they can move on. This is a crucial part of ear development (aural skills).

Developing and Using the Jazz Language

Having students sing jazz rhythms and patterns is a very effective way to have them learn to transcribe, whether by playing along or writing. In order to learn how to do this, your students need to be able to link jazz syllables to jazz written patterns. In jazz, a two-eighth-note pattern is not played as two equal notes. The first note will be long, and the second note will be short. The syllables most used are doo for the first note and bay for the second note. A four-beat pattern of eight eighth notes would be doo-bay doo-bay doo-bay doo-bay. A pattern of two eighths and a quarter note would be doo-bay bop, because quarter notes in jazz are short unless they are indicated as tenuto notes. In that case they become doo-bay ta or da (ta is better because it indicates that the note will be tongued). Marcato notes sound like shop or bop whether they are eighth notes or quarter notes. Staccato notes will also have the syllable shop or bop. Tenuto quarter notes will be ta. For example, four tenuto/legato quarter notes can be ta ta ta ta or what jazz players call lazy tongue da da da da. Once again, ta is preferred because it reminds students that each note must be tongued.

Students may also develop their own syllable vocabulary as long as the syllables are consistent with whether the notes are to be played long or short. A jazz improviser should think of developing improvisational skills as learning a new language. When you learned to speak, you learned words that were important to your very existence, and then you learned words that improved your quality of life. As you matured you moved from simple statements to more sophisticated statements. You used words and statements that had a logical flow together. You didn't jump from monosyllabic words to multisyllabic words. Most of your speech development depended on you listening to others speak. You chose parents, friends, relatives, and mentors as models for your speech. Before you learned to read or write, you learned the language you spoke completely from listening. The same principle is applied to everything stated above. Children who are developing language skills don't start with multisyllabic words that they don't understand. They use words from their current vocabulary. Novice improvisers should become fluent using notes, lines, and phrases that they understand. Remember, they are trying to tell a story. Good storytellers speak coherently. They don't suddenly throw in words that are big when simpler words go better with their story. The same must apply to improvisers when they are telling their story. The listener should be able to hear the natural flow of the improvised solo.

So how do you learn the jazz language besides listening to it? You start by developing facility on your instrument. You do digital exercises and arpeggios so that when you listen you can attempt to play what you've heard. Method books aren't intended to teach you to improvise. They are designed to help you develop the skills you'll need to improvise. If you have your students use method books, compare them with dictionaries. Dictionaries don't teach you how to write, they give you words and word meanings that help you use the best words to make your point. Method books serve the same purpose, they offer you good choices for what you want to play. Your students can use patterns in the method book and adjust them to fit their purpose and needs (that may mean substituting notes or rhythms to tweak the patterns). The idea behind everything that has been said in this chapter is to help the students be less intimidated and fearful in order to develop as improvisers. One of the biggest problems in teaching jazz improvisation is getting the novice improviser to relax and let the music flow naturally. The problem starts with the improviser's fear of failure, whether self-imposed or unwittingly imposed by the teacher/director.

Novice improvisers being compared to babies is not far off. Babies learning to walk don't fear falling until experience or adult reactions show them the dangers of falling. Improvisers can be traumatized by their first "fall." Your reaction as the director will either cause them to dust themselves off and try again or to slink into a corner feeling defeated. Encouraging words or reactions will help them recover and try again. Once again, avoid any words or reactions that may stifle your students' growth as improvisers.

Baby Steps

Continuing the baby analogy, the best thing to associate with novice improvisers is the progression from simple to difficult. Babies don't just suddenly start walking or running, they start by taking baby steps. They take slow steps to make sure that they won't fall and hurt themselves. They weigh out each step very carefully and methodically. They don't just assume that they can walk; they feel their way out at first. Improvisers do the same thing musically. Falling on your face literally and figuratively can cause pain. Babies get comforted after they fall, and that encouragement causes them to get up and try again. Novice improvisers are the same way. If you use encouraging words and actions your students won't develop the fear that stifles creativity. Have the students play the root note for each chord for the length indicated rhythmically. If there's one chord per measure, have them play one note for the number of counts indicated by the time signature (whole note for four counts in 4/4 time, etc.). Next, have them play two notes per chord as they listen carefully to the chord progressions. Once they are comfortable, have them play arpeggios on quarter notes or eighth notes. When they are comfortable with that, they can connect the arpeggios with scale tones or leading tones.

Creating Melodic Lines

As stated earlier, improvisation is creating variations on the theme or melody. Use the melody as a starting point for creating variations. The melody can be an anchor or checking point to make sure that the student stays on key and inside the form. When the student weaves in and out of the melody, they become aware of the tonal center. Subconsciously they are linked to the chord progressions without realizing it or thinking about it. This is what you hope to achieve during aural development. While performing jazz, things are happening too fast for conscious thought. There has to be a combination of muscle memory and aural awareness to put together a good improvised solo. If the student has not developed fluidity playing musical lines, it doesn't matter what they are hearing: their fingers won't be able to keep up. Most improvisers who fail can't put their fingers and ears together. They become frustrated, and that prevents them from being in the moment. Once they make a mistake, they can't recover. They spend time thinking about the mistake rather than moving on. Improvisers must be able to shake off mistakes because generally the "mistake" is not a note that sounds bad, it's simply not the note they wanted to play. Recovery and a determination to find the "right note" help improvisers. John Coltrane and Charlie Parker would play the same pattern in different places until they were satisfied that they had the right fit over the changes. They did it with lightning speed! Reading transcriptions of solos by the great jazz players helps you and your students understand what goes on while great players play.

Beyond Baby Steps

Facility on the instrument helps players move forward. As was mentioned previously, the reason most improvisers fail is that their fingers can't get to the notes their ears are hearing. Improvisers must have scales and arpeggios under their fingers. This means spending hours learning scales, modes, and arpeggios (chords, for piano and guitar). Students should use a metronome to practice scales, modes, and arpeggios to develop a sense of time and fluidity. Once again, this process should start slowly and methodically in order to achieve a comfort level and accuracy. Students tend to try to play things fast and stumble through things that are going to be important for fluid playing. The adage "Anything you can play well slowly, you'll be able to play fast" is true. Because you can't "unlearn" bad habits and mistakes, it's important that you don't develop them in the first place. It takes less time to learn something correctly than it does to go back and try to correct mistakes. What generally happens is the player becomes insecure and inhibited. This creates fear of failure, and that fear is difficult for players to overcome.

Learning to Overcome the Fear of Failure

It may sound cliché but success overcomes failure. Put your young improvisers in a position to succeed in their first attempt to solo. Remind them that they are telling a story through notes rather than words. They will hear "trigger tones," which are notes that lead them to the next notes or phrase in their solo. Sometimes these are notes they didn't mean to play but that get them from point A to point B. Trigger notes or leading tones are logical steps that take the improviser from one chord to the next. If the student used the "baby steps" approach and played the chord root notes, their ear subconsciously would learn the progressions. Their ear hears the logical progression from chord to chord, and their fingers just need to move to the notes the ear is directing them to. The more they listen to the song, the more comfortable they will become. The more comfortable they become, the better they will play. If you record them in class and have them record themselves during practice sessions, they will hear the progress they are making. They will hear the choices they made, and they will hear what would've been better choices.

Performance Time

If you've prepared your students to overcome the fear of failure, they should be ready for a real performance. During the performance you transition from teacher to cheerleader. You want to encourage them and give looks of approval to them. Even if they make poor note choices, the performance is not the place to correct them or make them aware of their mistakes. All this will do is discourage them from taking risks. Improvisers are supposed to take chances, try something that will breathe life into the song being performed. Nobody wants lukewarm coffee and no one likes a "safe solo." The player may make safe note choices, but they will have a bland solo. No "mistakes" were made, but without taking chances, the creativity is nonexistent. Most people prefer to hear the improviser experiment and problem solve on the spot rather than play it safe. The soloist should draw the listener into the adventure they're going on! Risk-taking is a valuable part of improvisation and a perfect solo will never be achieved, but that doesn't mean it shouldn't be attempted. Jazz players often say that they are always searching for the right note.

6

Planning Your First Performance

The previous chapters in this book have brought you to this point—the importance of a successful first performance. Unlike your band, your jazz ensemble will generally have one player per part. That means that each player will need to be able to carry their part. In a later chapter you'll find technology and software aids that will help you prepare individual students to practice and master basic skills needed for them to have a good performance. In this chapter we'll discuss the things that the group will need to be able to do as a whole.

The most important things the group needs to be able to do relate to articulation, intonation, stylistic interpretation, and clean attacks and releases (not necessarily in that order). What you do in your first rehearsal should apply directly to the first performance. Every skill you work on should be tailored to your needs for a good public performance.

With that in mind, attacks and releases should be worked on until you have clean attacks together and clean releases together. In no band group, classical or jazz, should students be allowed to enter early or late or cut off early or late. Precision is of the utmost importance. If you allow your students to be sloppy or relaxed on entrances and cutoffs in the rehearsal, they will do the same in performances. Take as much time as you need to achieve precise starts and precise endings to phrases and the entire song. There's no such thing as "close enough for jazz." Your students will resist and complain at first, but if you record your first rehearsal they will be able to hear how bad sloppy performances sound to audiences. All you will need to do is play the recording for them and highlight the places that need improvement.

As you work on your warmup piece, point out sloppy attacks and releases and intonation problems. Technology is such now that every student can download a tuning app and work on personal intonation outside of class. Have them use the tuner at the beginning of class and periodically during class. Using long tones is the best way to develop a good airflow and a good tone sound. Long tones will affect airflow, which will affect intonation and attacks and releases. Students need to be told the relationship between airflow and intonation, and airflow on attacks and releases. Be careful to remind them not to stop the sound with their tongue.

Cross listening is the key to everything that makes a good ensemble good. You can't play in tune with others if you can't hear them. You want students to listen for others playing the same part they are playing and parts that are harmonizing with them, and for those who are playing a phrase that will lead to the phrase they will be playing. Compare passing phrases with relay races. The person receiving the baton in a relay race must be prepared for a seamless passing of the baton (the release) and then a seamless acceptance of and carrying of the baton (the attack and playing of the next phrase). This provides a visual in their minds, and they can relate to a dropped baton or a sloppy handoff.

Writing Lesson Plans for Jazz Class

Lesson plans for jazz ensemble should be stated in behavioral terms. As mentioned before, they should have clear and specific goals and outcomes. Some of the teaching objectives include working on intonation, articulation, tone quality, expression, rhythmic patterns, and overall jazz interpretation. Your lesson plans should state how you will focus on each of these elements and what techniques you will use to teach them. As stated previously, every jazz class should start with a warmup that works on or reinforces jazz styles. You need to work every day on a new technique or style that relates to the music you will be working on. Your plans need to be spelled out with specific goals and expected outcomes. A good performance depends on good preparation and good preparation has to be well planned.

Lesson plans should contain the following: the stated objective in behavioral terms (today we will work on "Satin Doll," making sure we achieve 100% accuracy on attacks and releases) and a statement on how you will achieve your goal and how you will apply your techniques to ensure an accurate performance. Each part of the plan should be specific, not generalized.

The Performance

There are many moving parts to the performance. Your students should know that the performance begins with them taking the stage and ends with their exiting the stage. Most students will think that playing the music is the performance. Unfortunately, a lot of directors think the same way. A disorganized entrance or exit taints the audience's view of the overall performance. Students should have uniform folders, and they should be dressed the same way (as simple as wearing white tops and black bottoms). Most music stores offer folders to schools free or for a minimal charge. White dress tops and black pants and shoes are normal performance attire, tuxedos and black dresses for formal attire. Whatever you decide to wear, everyone should be uniformly dressed.

Walking onto the stage should be organized. The rhythm section should go on first to set up and tune up. Then each section should enter in the order of their seating. Exiting the stage should be the opposite order of entering the stage. Better groups concentrate on professional looking entrances and exits. Reacting as a group begins with the simple act of uniformity entering the stage area. Students must focus their attention as a group.

Once the group is onstage, the group should be focused on the performance of the music. There should be no talking, and the group should be ready to play a tuning note: Concert F, B♭, or A. They should have pretuned before coming onstage, so this will be a tuning check and a check of the room's acoustics. Once the tuning is complete, their focus should be on you in preparation for the downbeat of the first song. Unlike in concert band, you can count off, snap, or clap the tempo. Between songs it's okay to check the tuning to avoid any group or sectional intonation problems.

If there are soloists in any tune (piece) you play, applaud them after they play, and at the end of the song, acknowledge them by name. For jazz performances it's acceptable for the audience to applaud soloists during the song. You can cue the audience by clapping and nodding at the soloists once they finish their solo. Remember, you're teaching the audience how to react to jazz performances.

Before starting the next song, take out time to look over the band (especially the rhythm section) to make sure everyone is ready for the next downbeat. Strings break, drum sticks drop, reeds break, valves and slides have problems that require immediate attention, and so on. You don't want to start your count off and then discover a problem—scan the band.

Keep in mind, the way your students feel about this first performance will affect all future performances. As was stated before, there is no such thing as "close enough" for jazz. The day after the first performance, you should evaluate the recording of the performance (audio or video). Before you critique the group, allow them to listen to the performance. Use a guided listening discussion to evaluate the pros and cons of the performance. Do not allow the students to refer to other students by name. Use terms like "the second alto came in late." Even though there's one person playing second alto and everyone knows their name, it isn't taken as a personal attack, and the player hears the importance of each part being played accurately.

At the end of the first performance, acknowledge the work you and your students did. Tell the audience that you did well but they as the audience can expect things to continue to get better as the year goes on. You're passively asking the audience to hold you and your students to a high standard, and you're not making excuses for any problems that may have happened. Because it's the first performance, no one, including you, should leave thinking that you reached your terminal objective. They should hear you as a good group on its way to becoming a better group.

Rehearse your group bowing and have them leave the stage in an organized manner. Don't allow your students to call out to the audience, wave, or do anything to detract from the good job they did during the performance. Remember, this first performance sets the tone for all future performances.

It may seem like showing your students proper stage decorum takes a lot of time, but once you establish your standards and expectations, they will rise to the occasion. In future performances they will remind their peers how to carry themselves professionally. If the performance is videotaped, during the next rehearsal evaluate the group's appearance as well as their sound. If the group looks uninterested during the performance, that affects how the audience reacts. You unwittingly tell the audience visually that they don't have to react positively to soloists or solos being played. Watching the group's body language will show you what needs to be addressed for future performances. Obviously, you don't want the members of the group talking while others are playing, and that tells the audience that talking during the performance is unacceptable.

The things discussed here may not seem necessary to teach your class, but they are very important for a successful performance. Catcalls from the audience and loud comments from the audience are unacceptable. Should they happen, it's important that you address them from the stage. You're introducing a whole new culture, and that means educating the audience as much as you have educated your students. Middle-school and high-school audiences may not have ever attended a jazz performance and need to be taught proper etiquette. Standing on stage teaching them proper reactions to what they are hearing is a validation for your students on the value of jazz and jazz performances.

Have your saxophone players take a backup reed onstage with them. Should their reed break, you don't want them sitting there not playing or having to leave the stage to retrieve a backup reed. Brass players should have slide oil or valve oil on their stands. Room temperatures can affect valves and slides, and because there's one player per part, you can't afford to lose a player because of a stuck valve or a sticky valve. "Be prepared and you won't panic" is the working motto. You don't want to have nonmusical things impact your performance. Panic and concern over reeds or valves can ruin a performance, because panic is contagious. You can rest assured that a reed will break and a valve will stick at the worst possible time. Plan for the worse but hope for the best.

7
Festival Preparation and Performance

Preparing for a festival or assessment is very much like preparing for your first performance but with a few obvious differences. First, by the time you start preparing for a festival/assessment, your group should have had one or two performances and be well rehearsed and prepared for adjudication. Second, unlike a concert, an assessment has three adjudicators listening to your performance and following a score to judge performance accuracy.

Festival Information and Description

Every state music association gives a description of the purpose of festivals and the importance of festival participation. In the description there's an explanation of festival grades. You should include the description and explanations in your band/jazz handbook so that your students and their parents can understand the importance of the festival. Generally, these festivals are not competitive on the local and state levels. Groups can receive ratings (Superior, Excellent, Good, Fair, and Poor) or receive comments only. During the performance the judges write and voice-record comments that describe the areas done well and those that need improvement. There is no winner or loser in these assessments. There are festivals on the national level that you can participate in that are competitive. The judges use the same criteria for judging but assign numeric values to each category. The numbers are tallied, and first, second, or third place are awarded based on the top three highest scores.

You should impart your personal view of the importance of festival participation and why your students are required to participate. You will need to show the percentage of your students' grade that is associated with festival participation and that you expect 100 percent participation from your students. Your handbook should copy the explanation of ratings exactly as printed in the state association's festival handbook. To show the educational value of festivals, you should make it clear that your jazz ensemble's growth is not just determined by the final rating. The adjudicators only see a snapshot of what your jazz ensemble has done and judged based on a standard of performances they have witnessed or expected from personal experience. You and your group know how far along they've come and how well they performed based on their preparation.

Preparing to Be Adjudicated

On paper, preparing for a concert and preparing for adjudication involve the same things: performing attacks and releases accurately, good intonation, good balance, rhythmic accuracy, good articulation, and style accuracy. What is different are the standards for performing for an audience of untrained listeners versus performing for judges following the score. An audience won't normally know the difference between an accurate performance and an "okay" performance. Judges, from their experience and the benefit of having scores to follow, will know the difference.

Score Study

How well you as the director prepare before adjudication will determine how effective you are. Score study enables you to plan out the best way to teach the festival pieces to your students. Work through how you will present and rehearse the pieces with your group. Determine what sections of the pieces will be most challenging to your students and decide the best way you will present and rehearse these difficult and challenging parts. The more prepared and organized you are before the rehearsal, the more organized the rehearsal will be. If you come across parts that are beyond your scope of knowledge, seek out help or assistance. Contact another jazz director, former college instructor, or a private teacher or master musician if necessary. The bottom line is that if during your score study you discover your personal limitations, don't allow false pride to get in the way of you getting help.

Making Notes on the Score

Because the judges will have a score for each piece you'll be performing, you need to mark your scores so that you won't miss the challenging parts that they will see. Circle sections of the pieces that will need special attention. It may be that you need to give a cue or simply a reassuring look to help build confidence. Whatever the case may be, you'll want to be prepared so that you can prepare your students in advance. Don't give the judges your work score as one of the copies to use because it will provide them with a guide to recognize your problem areas or weaknesses. For teaching purposes, on your work score, write in the solutions you have for problem areas.

Teaching the Music for Adjudication

As you study the score, you should make notes for yourself to use to teach the music. These notes should offer a step-by-step approach to use as a teaching plan for your lesson plans. The lesson plan will state what your goal is in general, and these notes will be your complete description of the way you plan to achieve the goal and execute your plan. Unlike the lesson plan that's written for nonmusicians to be able to follow, your teaching notes will be more detailed and use terminology musicians use in preparing for a performance.

One of the first and most important parts of teaching music for adjudication is that from the beginning, you must address everything in the score. You don't learn notes and rhythms first and come back and learn dynamics and expression; you learn everything first time through. If you sight-read the pieces before you start the process of teaching them, it's okay not to stop for items being missed or overlooked. You'll be preparing your students for the skills they'll need for sight-reading, which is an important part of the festival. Sight-reading without stopping will give you a chance to identify problem areas in the music that you may not have recognized as problems during your score study.

When you begin the process of teaching the music, you must choose your words carefully. You don't want to inadvertently create problems or cause your students to develop insecurities or fears of difficult parts. Frustration breeds frustration, so it's important that you don't allow any fears you may have to be transmitted to your group by your word choices. Always go from the familiar to the unfamiliar. Start with what your students know about the style, period, and different performance practices from similar pieces. This is why selecting music for the first rehearsal is so important. If you choose music for the first rehearsal that is consistent with the skills required for good jazz playing, you can expand on those skills for the adjudication pieces.

The following should be your "playbook" for preparing for a festival:

1. Be methodical. Make sure you don't select large chunks of the music to teach in each class period. Based on the level of difficulty and how meticulous you'll need to be, allot yourself enough time to give thorough explanations and for your students to put your explanations to use. Don't leave a section until the students have acquired the skills needed and have performed it at a satisfactory level.

2. Locate sections in the piece you're working on that may appear in the music for different jazz ensemble sections. If the first and second trumpets have the same material in different parts of the music, teach it to them both at the same time. If they have the same part but in different keys, teach them the rhythms, phrasing, articulations, and other items that are the same. If you can teach multiple sections the same melodic lines or parts at the same time, you won't have to worry about students getting bored and having discipline problems (boredom is the main reason for discipline problems in jazz groups).
3. Have students clap, pat, or sing challenging rhythms. Once again, in most of the music you choose, you'll find that melodies travel throughout the ensemble. During your score study you should've discovered this. Trace the melodies and counter parts and bring them to the attention of your students. There will be students in each section who will be able to identify the similarities in their parts and the parts of other sections, so solicit their help in assisting their classmates. Have these students point to the section where they hear the melodic lines being played. After they do that, have only the sections that have the melody play. Without any other parts playing, have the students playing the melody match the dynamics of the section that played the melody before. Emphasize the point that it should sound like one continuous line with no measurable breaks. Next, have the full ensemble play and adjust their dynamics in such a way that the melody can be heard. Compare the passing off of the melody with the passing of the baton in a relay race.
4. Use long tones to demonstrate the phrase shapes and dynamics. Before playing a two-measure or four-measure phrase, have the group play a long tone the length of the phrase and follow the crescendo and decrescendo markings. Be sure to emphasize that the diminuendo/decrescendo should start at a stronger level than it ends and not suddenly get soft. Too many groups play subito (sudden change) rather than a gradual change. Adjudicators

know that this is a common problem for jazz ensembles, and when they hear an ensemble execute it properly, they know it's something that has been discussed in class.
5. Follow period-accurate articulations. Remember, short/detached notes are played differently in different styles and periods (Dixieland, swing, bebop, and Latin).

Once you have concluded the preceding steps, the group can play through the piece section by section following all markings. Pacing of the lesson is important, because trying to rush through the piece to cover a lot in one rehearsal may mean overlooking important details. Working too slow can cause your students to become bored and turned off to important details you're trying to bring to their attention. Many directors have difficulty determining the pace at which student learning should take place. There's no exact formula, because students will have varying abilities. Deciding when to press on with a lesson and when to pull up is difficult. You should gain a sense of your group and know when to step away from your quest for perfection.

One solution for pacing is deciding on how to break your lesson/rehearsal into manageable units. Trying to achieve too much too soon can be counterproductive. Students can be discouraged or overwhelmed if you try to do too much in one rehearsal. They may leave class thinking they have failed because they didn't achieve what they thought they should have. During your score study, you should've decided exactly what parts of the piece pose the greatest challenges. Aim for a reasonable amount of time to spend on specific sections of the piece. During the rehearsal, be willing to scale down on the lesson. Try to recognize the body language and facial expressions of your students to know when it's time to move on. This doesn't mean to leave something incomplete; it means that if you must spend more time to get something right, you should leave the piece or work on something less demanding. Once again, keep a realistic sense of what you can accomplish. In the early days of the ensemble, you may have to simplify parts for some of your players. There's nothing wrong with that as long as you maintain the integrity of the piece.

Record Your Rehearsals

So that your students know what they need to work on, record your rehearsals. Sometimes students think you're just going over pieces they play well and they don't try to make corrections. Record them and then do a guided listening exercise using the adjudication sheets the judges will use. Play the recording for them to comment on, with no comments from you. Let them be the adjudicators. After they have made their comments, play the recording again and make your comments. Have the students read their comments on each adjudicated category (tone quality, balance, articulation, etc.). Encourage the students not to make their comments personal but to refer to specific sections of the group and piece. For example, "The saxophones didn't play the diminuendo in measures four through eight effectively," or "The rhythm section needs to increase their volume in section A for us to have a better balance." You may be surprised at how much your students will hear once they assume the position of adjudicator. Immediately after listening to the recording, have the group play through the piece they critiqued, and record it. Compare the two recordings and then decide if they made enough of a difference in the second performance of the piece to obtain a higher grade. In most cases, this exercise will make students more aware of what has to be done on a daily basis to achieve a successful festival/adjudication performance.

8

Developing a Jazz Budget Separate from the Band Budget

Even though you may have experience developing a budget for your band program, it's not necessarily true that you'll know how to develop a budget for jazz. Because jazz bands use electronic instruments and maintenance and repairs of electronic equipment can be quite expensive, you will need more funds. This chapter provides information that will be important for you to know how to accurately budget for needs and program growth. Depending on the size of your jazz group, jazz band expenses can be included in an instrumental music program budget.

In the early years of the development of your jazz program, you should meet with your principal and explain what your vision of your program is and what kinds of financial resources you'll need for it to be successful. Jazz programs bring a lot of positive attention to schools, and you should make your principal aware of the benefits of having a well-funded program in your school. Because principals have discretionary funds they can tap into to develop new programs and start new projects, you should have a list of needs to lay out that explain expected expenses. The more money you can get from the school, the less you'll need to raise. Your principal will also know of available program development funds available to schools for new program development from the district or state level (this is especially important for Title I schools).

After meeting with your principal, you should take a needs inventory. If there has never been a jazz ensemble in your school, you'll need to purchase at least one string bass or an electric bass, a bass amplifier, a guitar amplifier, an electric keyboard, and one complete drum set. If you're not sure what your needs will be, consult a director of an established program to find out what your starter needs and your five-year needs will be. It will be better to spend your money developing your program than saving money that may be lost in the next fiscal year. School budgets are decided based on your past purchase record. Leftover funds may be cut from future budgets.

Your school business manager or financial secretary should have a bid list for purchases with vendors you'll be ordering from. This list will enable you to find "must have" items for your program. The list will make developing a realistic budget possible, but you should not budget to the exact price total. You must have room for price increases so that your budget does not fall short. Once you develop a budget, you may not be able to go back for more funds if you are under budget. A business manager once said that every budget can be cut by 33 percent. Knowing this, budget over by 33 percent in order to get the amount you need.

Music purchases and method books should be your number-one priority. These purchases can sometimes be paid for through textbook allocations since sheet music and method books are vital to music instruction. Your budget should include funds for method books and sheet music for a forty-five minute performance. You will also need a digital recording system and an audio system for guided listening activities.

Most schools provide funds for classroom materials such as pencils, chalk, paper, and items needed for instructional use. It's difficult to separate instructional needs from performance needs since jazz band is a performance group. For this reason, your budget will contain items that are provided by the school (paper, pencils, copying costs, etc.).

Developing a Jazz Budget Separate from the Band Budget / 65

The following is a sample of the kinds of items your budget should include. Since every school district is unique, you may have to add or subtract items. The intent here is not to provide an absolute budget; it is only to provide you with an outline of expected expenditures so that you may calculate the income needed to maintain your program:

- Supplies and Materials: photocopy and printing paper, music notation pads, workbooks, pencils, markers, and notation software
- Maintenance: for amplifiers; audiovisual equipment; office equipment, including repairs; music stands, including replacement; and piano tuning
- Festival/Assessment: registration fees, bus rental, solo and ensemble fees, extra score purchases, festival music purchases
- Equipment Replacement/Purchases: inventory replacement needs, music stands, chairs, music storage cabinets, video-streaming systems, audio systems, instrument storage cages, recording equipment, and engraved music folders
- Travel Expenses: transportation costs for local and out-of-town festivals and activities.

After you have listed ongoing budgetary expenses, start listing expenses that will be unique to the current school year. Once you have taken an inventory of school-owned instruments and equipment, take an inventory of unused materials and supplies. Don't spend money on things you already have enough of. The money you save can be contingency funds for unexpected expenses. Consult your band budget to gain a feel for the total amount of funds needed. Within two years of existence, new programs will have the same expenses that established programs incur. This is where your experience developing a band budget will come in handy. The life and success of your program will depend on how well you develop your operating budget.

Remember, in order to effectively establish a working budget, it is important that you outline expected income and expenditures. Contact colleagues personally or through social media to get information on expenses you may not be aware of. Once again, after you submit your requests for funding assistance, you may not be able to submit a new request or submit an amended request. Research carefully and completely so that once you submit your budget request, it will cover all of your needs and expenses. Facebook has several band director and jazz director groups that you can post questions to or ask for tips or assistance.

Since your students will need concert attire, you may or may not need to purchase outfits for your students or assist students who can't afford to purchase outfits. Sometimes there are parents in the program who can make outfits or accessories for your group. Before you complete your budget, you should find out how much your attire will cost each student and determine how much of those costs you'll need to include in your budget. Remember, bow ties and other ties will get lost, jackets and pants may be ripped, shirts and blouses may get scorched by an iron. You'll need to replace or fix damaged items, so you'll need funds at your discretion to do that. If students are expected to cover lost, stolen, or damaged outfits, that should be clearly stated in your handbook.

Travel Expenses

Travel outside of the school district or state falls into two categories: student costs and school costs. Your budget must include funds for students who need assistance. Since jazz ensembles have one person per part in most cases, you'll need everyone to travel for competitions and assessments. Not every student will be able to afford to pay for a trip, so your budget has to have funds to assist these students. One way to help is to have fundraisers that allow students to raise money for their own personal account. You can have a percentage of the fundraiser go into the general account for your budget and a percentage into the student account. Your budget should include the amounts separated so that there is no confusion. Parents generally don't like for money they raise to go toward a student account that's not their child's account. As you explain this part of your budget, make the percentages clear to avoid any confusion. Before choosing a fundraiser, be sure you know how much money will be needed per student and chaperone for you to be able to afford the trip. Work backward from the total cost to the total need. You'll need funds in your budget to cover basic needs and travel costs. Obviously, if you can't raise the funds for the trip without impacting your budget you shouldn't plan the trip.

Electronic Equipment

As mentioned earlier, the purchasing of electronic equipment is going to be one of the biggest costs in your budget. Amplifiers, microphones, audio-playback equipment, video-recording equipment, and recording software are the basic needs. Microphone stands, cables, and electronic tuners will also be needed. Fortunately, the purchases you make in the first year will last for at least five years, so you'll only need to annually budget for maintenance, repairs, and replacement. Secure bids and get recommendations from colleagues about what brands are best for your needs. Since jazz bands travel, durability is of the utmost importance. Things may seem expensive, but when you consider their durability, the cost is relative. Equipment that lasts is a smarter buy than having to replace things annually because you chose a less expensive, lower-quality item. Remember, buy things that you expect to last at least five years. There will be parts of the drum set that may need to be replaced annually, and strings and bass bridges need to be budgeted for annually. Budget developers suggest that you budget 30 percent higher than your expected needs to cover unexpected needs.

Before you purchase recording equipment (microphones, mixers, and software), check with recording professionals and colleagues to make sure you get the items that best suit your needs. All equipment you purchase for jazz ensembles should be items that you can transport with you for out-of-school performances. There are recording packages that you can purchase that are designed to be used in school or remotely (set up away from your school). Decide on your needs. Are you planning on streaming your performances? Are you going to use the equipment in class for guided listening exercises? Do you need microphones, stands, and cables? Are you going to make CDs (some schools still use CDs)? These questions need to be addressed before you make a purchase. There are handheld devices that can make a good recording and there are different microphones that make the highest-quality recordings. Your budget will determine which is best for you. During your first year you should get the highest-quality equipment possible. This is why it was suggested previously that you meet with your principal to determine how much of the cost for establishing the program your school and your school district will cover. Your budget should not be expected to cover the initial cost for establishing the program. Include in the budget you propose to your principal all of the costs you expect annually and the amount you consider to be program establishment costs. Your annual budget after the establishment cost is not going to be the same every year.

9

Program Maintenance

After you have started your program and established standards, you'll need to take steps to maintain and grow your program. Planning and setting goals are very important in this process. Your mission statement, philosophy of music, unit plans, and daily lesson plans are intricate parts of your program maintenance as well as program development. Good planning and management are vital parts of the process of maintaining your program. Students don't want to be in classes that they feel are a waste of their time. Positive word of mouth from students is a positive recruiting tool, and students who enjoy class activities tend to stay.

Developing a Five-Year Plan

Having a five-year plan is like having a GPS system for your program. For programs to be maintained, you'll need well-functioning equipment, a full library of music, good storage areas, and of course, students. As you set program goals, you need to make sure they're consistent with your philosophy of teaching. Your philosophy should state what you want to do as an educator. What do you want your jazz students to gain from working with you? What resources do you need to achieve your personal goals? Your goals will guide what you want your students to achieve. Once you're clear on what you want to achieve as a professional, you can then decide what you want your program to achieve. Visualize the end product first, and then plan how you want to achieve the finished product.

Your five-year plan should have specific goals and a timeline for completing those goals. The stronger the foundation, the stronger the finished product. The plan should involve teaching goals, basic management, and planning for equipment and instrument purchases. You should plan for recruitment, retention, and reclaiming. Even though you want to recruit well in the first two years, you want to devote most of your efforts to maintaining the students you have. In the unfortunate case you lose students for whatever reason, you want to have a plan in place to reclaim any students you lose. There are usually signs that students don't plan to remain in your program, and if you keep your fingers on the pulse of your group, you can encourage those contemplating leaving to stay. Address those issues in your five-year plan. There are basically two reasons students leave a new program—boredom or being overwhelmed by difficult music. Classroom management should not be one of the reasons students leave. Good planning on your part should avoid classroom management issues or disciplinary problems that turn students off.

Purchasing and Maintaining Equipment

During the first year of your program, there will be purchases you have to make to help establish the program. As mentioned before, there will be very few students who own a string bass (transporting these instruments to and from school is a major problem). In order to make sure your students can play these instruments in class, you will need to purchase them for the school. Of course, if you purchase the instruments, you will also need to purchase storage racks to hold them. As you build your music library you will need file cabinets and storage bins for folders. You'll need storage cages or storage shelves to hold guitars, basses, and drum set equipment.

As you begin to make purchases and stock your program, contact jazz directors and ask them to help you acquire the things that you will need. It's one thing to get things that are recommended and another thing to get things that are vital. You'll need a recording and playback system for your students to hear and track their progress. After every performance and some rehearsals, you will need to have guided listening sessions for your students to evaluate what they have done and need to do. Just telling them won't always connect because they may feel that you are just being hard on them. Once you guide them through listening and evaluating the performance, they will begin to hear their successes and failures. Getting them to be actively involved in the evaluation process gets them to buy into the process and not get turned off because they don't think they can please you. Listening to themselves provides them with the opportunity to self-evaluate. If you don't actively take part in the evaluation process, they will problem solve. You will maintain your high standards, and they will adopt your views because they will hear things that need to be polished if not corrected.

The Importance of Individual Recognition and Praise

One of the best ways to keep students in your program is to recognize individual or small-group achievements. There are many ways to do this, from posting on your group's social media pages or school website to posting pictures on school walls or in the band room. Take a picture of the individual or group and post it as a student spotlight, player of the week, or section/ensemble of the week. The esteem of the recipient(s) will rise, and other students will aspire to achieve such recognition. This will create the kind of environment in which players will want to remain. You can leave the pictures on a bulletin board or on the website all year. At the end of the year, you can select a Section of the Year or Most Valuable Player Award. Students who are coming to the school or your program for the first time will notice that they can be recognized for their achievements and see that they will be valued in your program. This means so much for recruiting and retaining for your program.

Some schools still have printed newsletters that they send home with students. There should never be a week that passes that there's not something positive about your students and/or your program in it. The PTSA (Parent Teacher Student Association) in most schools use a listserv email system to disseminate information about the school. Have the publicity committee of your parent group profile a student or ensemble each week. Remember, if students feel valued, they will stay in your program and will be more apt to encourage other students to join. The best way not to have to reclaim students is not to lose them in the first place. You should also send positive information about your program to the middle school(s) and elementary school(s). Your five-year plan will include these students as future members, and if they see positive information about your program, their interests will develop.

Don't just recognize students who have obvious accomplishments; that won't really help your program grow. You should have an award and recognition for students who contribute to your program but are not the most talented. These students who are in "supporting roles" can receive an "unsung hero" type of reward. The top players will always return to your program, but the players who work hard behind the scenes won't return unless they know their participation is appreciated. This may sound cliché, but you're a teacher first. It's your responsibility to reach every student and create a nurturing environment.

The more aware you are of the human dynamic involved, the more you will succeed. Recognition is equated with value, and the more you recognize your students, the more valued they will feel. Students who work on improvisation should be profiled for their achievements even if they haven't improvised on a public performance. These students can be rewarded for being most improved players or courageous jazz warriors for arming themselves with the needed skills for jazz performance. Jazz without improvisation is not considered jazz by many jazz performers, so if you have students working on improvisation, it is essential that they be recognized. If you have a year-end awards program, be mindful that it's not about the size of the award but the fact that you are recognizing student achievement.

Having your students recognize student achievements builds the team spirit needed for your program to grow in quantity and quality. Peer recognition is one of your most powerful retention aids. Knowing that they are respected by their peers for their hard work motivates students to do their best. Applause from audiences is great, but applause and recognition from those who know the challenges of what they're doing is invaluable. Never underestimate the importance of peer acceptance. Music groups thrive on social interaction; not wanting to let the group down is a powerful motivator for practice. As was mentioned earlier in the book, because jazz ensembles generally have one person per part, each person is very important for the group's success. The old adage "You're only as strong as your weakest link" is very true. One ill-prepared player can ruin a performance, so positive reinforcement can inspire and encourage weaker players to work hard to improve. Criticism without encouragement is counterproductive. Having others in the group or school to recognize even small achievements is a big help in building individual confidence.

In order to keep students engaged and in your program, you will need to motivate and reward individual students. During class, recognize students who have improved because of out-of-class practice. Public praise is good, but pulling a student aside to tell them that you have noticed their improvement is very important. This shows that you value their contributions to the group, and it also acknowledges individual growth. A third-chair player should see themselves as an important contributing member of the group. Even though this is an individual acknowledgement, it is also a team-building exercise. The group can only be as strong as its individual members. Students who are not actively involved in improving themselves cannot improve the group.

If you have advanced students in the group, another way of recognizing their talent is to form a combo or use homogeneous duos, trios, or quartets. These more advanced students can show their individual abilities through a smaller, more focused group. One of the benefits of using smaller groups is that the things they develop in the smaller group can be transferred to the larger group. In a combo, improvisation is the focus. In homogeneous groups, phrasing, intonation, and attacks and releases are the focus. All of the skills needed for success in the smaller group are also important in the larger group. Listening is the most important skill that will be developed. When you program them for a performance, you can spend time praising them for their achievements and hard work. This kind of recognition motivates other members of the larger group to work with smaller groups in the ensemble and build the required skills to succeed as a jazz player.

10

Using Technology in the Jazz Classroom

Before going out and spending money from your budget on the latest electronic gear, decide what you want to achieve by using the new technology. Some ways of using technology in the jazz classroom will be to use it for recording and replay, tuning, listening to audio recordings, watching video recordings, videoconferencing with guest artists who can't physically come into the classroom, and a host of other helpful activities. Here are a few suggestions for using technology in the jazz classroom.

Recording Your Group

Probably the most valuable way to use technology in your classroom is recording your group. Making the best recording is more than putting one or two microphones in front of your group and pressing "Record." The object of making a recording is to give your students an opportunity to hear what you hear. The recording should be clear and balanced so that your students can critique themselves and understand what you've been talking about. You want them to hear the effects of sloppy attacks and releases and intonation problems. If you have quality recording and playback equipment, your students can hear what you have been telling them is good and what needs improvement.

The book *Recording Tips for Music Educators* (Oxford University Press) goes into detail about different recording techniques, equipment that should be purchased, and how to set up your equipment to get the best recording. This chapter will take a cursory look at a few ways to record in your classroom.

There are four basic setups for using microphones to record jazz groups large and small. The first is to use a parallel pair of microphones placed in front of the ensemble on a fifteen-foot microphone stand. The best microphones to use are condenser microphones with a cardioid pattern, but a pair of dynamic microphones can also be used. The next configuration is the X/Y pattern, also on a fifteen-foot stand placed directly behind the conductor facing down at the group. Like the parallel pair, the X/Y setup provides a stereo pattern that imitates what the human ear hears.

Another setup used is called mid-side recording. Mid-side uses a mid-microphone, which has a cardioid pattern aimed at the sound source, and a bidirectional microphone used to capture sound from the sides. Like the parallel pair, mid-side attempts to capture sound in the way the human ear does.

The last of the four is used for larger jazz ensembles. It's called the Decca Tree setup. The Decca Tree uses three microphones: one facing left, one facing center, and one facing right. You can also add two outlying microphones (one on each corner of the stage). Since you don't have three ears, the purpose of this setup is to give you a surround sound effect that enables you to record every sound equally. Consult a recording professional for assistance with these setups and advice on the best recording console to purchase.

If you don't want to purchase microphones and recording consoles, there's technology that can fit in your pocket and can be used instead of microphones. These devices are handheld recording devices. They have built-in microphones that can be configured into parallel patterns or X/Y patterns. The advantage of using handheld recording devices is that you can use free downloadable software to prepare your recording for replay for your students. Zoom, the leading manufacturer of handheld devices, makes microphones that can be used with iPhones and iPads. You can play back your recording on any Bluetooth compatible devices. The drop in quality from using microphones is slight, but the advantage of handhelds is that you can place them on a microphone stand in front of the group and get a representative recording for your group. Smartphones and tablets have microphones for recording, but the quality of the recording is not as high as with microphones and handheld devices (unless you attach an external microphone or Zoom adapter microphone to them).

Some groups record with the idea of streaming their performances or formatting the recording to be sold. Before you record and distribute recordings, you must secure the rights to record and distribute all of the music you plan to record. If you sell recordings with any copyrighted music that you don't have clearance for, you are in violation of US copyright laws. The Harry Fox Agency (HFA Songfile), ASCAP, and BMI have databases you can search for publishing rights and secure permissions and clearances.

Using Tablets and Smartphones

There are many uses, other than for recording, for smartphones and tablets in jazz classes. There are lots of tuning apps and metronome apps that can be downloaded for free. You should find the one best suited for your group's use and have your students download them for use.

Tablets and smartphones are handheld computers and give your students instant access to the internet. If you're preparing program notes on the pieces you're working on in class, you can have your students use a search engine to locate the information. This gives them valuable insight into the composer, the period, the style, and the performance characteristics of the piece. Students are able to be active participants in the history of the piece(s) you've chosen.

Music on a Tablet

Many music publishers are currently making music available for download onto tablets. This helps avoid torn or frayed music, lost music, and music too small for some students to see. Stage lighting is not an issue since tablet lighting can be adjusted to meet the players' needs. Another advantage of music on a tablet is that you and your students always have access to individual parts, there are no shared folders. Leather-bound folders can be expensive, and if a student loses the folder, you have the expense of replacing the folder and all of the music contained in it. If a tablet is lost, you can download the music onto another tablet. Smartphones can also download music, but because of the size of the screen, they are not practical for use during performances.

Interactive Software

One of the most used technologies in the band and orchestra classroom is Smartmusic. Smartmusic is an interactive music software program designed to go along with music instruction. Students receive immediate feedback on their playing and discover areas that need improvement. You can use Smartmusic for seating placement, to test playing, and to monitor practice. Students can learn scales, develop sight-reading skills, and study the jazz pieces you're working on in class. Smartmusic keeps students engaged in the learning process even when their part is not displayed. Smartmusic is a web-based platform with a huge library of music that enables you to create individualized lessons/assignments for every student. It provides a tuner, a metronome, practice exercises, and some of the requirements some states have for scales. The built-in notation tools allow teachers to create, edit, and import content for their students. Your students receive immediate feedback as they practice each assignment. You are able to receive their best performance of assignments so you can grade them. Your students can work on specific assignments from you and submit their best work for you to grade.

Play-Along Recordings

Before Smartmusic became available, Jamey Aebersold developed "Play-A-Long" vinyl records. As technology developed, they became digital recordings. DAT recordings, CDs, and video recordings can also be used in your classroom or your students' homes so that they can develop improvisation skills. Music Minus One and other play-along formats can be used too.

Using standard jazz literature and blues with a jazz rhythm section, these play-along recordings enable your students to play along in order to develop their improvisation skills or just learn and practice jazz melodies. The Jamey Aebersold Play-A-Long catalog has hundreds of pieces ranging from jazz and blues standards, Latin pieces, fusion, and original pieces by some of the biggest names in jazz. You can also order transcribed solos that can be played with the play-along recordings. Hal Leonard has a series that provides sample solos written specifically for novice jazz players. Composers like Lennie Niehaus have solo books for improvisation that also include CDs for play-along. There's a wealth of material available, including things found in such jazz improvisation software as Band in a Box, Mapping Tonal Harmony Pro, and Garage Band. Do your research and find instructional materials best suited for you and your students.

Websites

The following websites are quite helpful for use in the jazz classroom:

  https://www.musictheory.net/
  https://www.musictechteacher.com/
  https://www.get-tuned.com/
  https://www.mdecks.com/

Social Media

There are so many ways to use social media to work with your jazz groups. All you need is a Bluetooth-enabled screen/monitor in your classroom. You can bring guest artists from anywhere in the world via Zoom, Google Meet, Skype, or FaceTime. This real-time interaction allows you to have your students perform live for and get immediate feedback from a clinician. The guest(s) can perform for your students so that they can model the sounds that they hear. Videoconferencing can be done with a group of guests at one time, so you can have every instrument in the jazz ensemble represented in one session. Manufacturers like Conn-Selmer, Vandoren, and D'Addario have a list of performing artists that will come to your classroom via videoconferencing or in person. Contact them or other such manufacturers to secure a professional who will demonstrate and interact with your group.

Facebook

Facebook has several groups dedicated to teaching jazz and teaching music. Using Messenger, you can interact with jazz teachers who can critique your group and make valuable observations. The largest group is Band Directors; it has members who are going through the same pains you'll be going through as a band director teaching jazz. There are several groups for jazz educators, jazz performers, and manufacturers who work with school jazz groups.

X (Formerly Twitter)

Similar to Facebook, X has members and groups that can be helpful to you and your students. You can keep up with new technology and find out which technology is best for you and your needs.

Google

Besides being a great search engine, Google actually has a lot of things that can help educators. You can get lesson plans and interactively engage with others in real time to customize lesson plans or get lesson ideas. Google Slides enable you to make visuals for your students to use. Google Meet enables you to interact with musicians via live video.

Notation Software

Notation software used in jazz classrooms serves three major purposes: it gives you the opportunity to rewrite or arrange parts for the group, allows you to print missing parts provided by publishing companies, and allows your students to compose and arrange. Music publishing companies have teamed with notation software companies to enable you to download and print parts you need from a huge database of songs. You may have to pay a minimal fee, but if you've purchased the music, some allow you to download a specified number of parts at no cost. As is the case with using tablets, you have the option of printing or downloading onto the tablet directly. Sibelius and Finale are the two most-used notation software programs, but there are several available on the market to match your budget needs. It doesn't matter if you have a music store with a large inventory of music near you. All you need do is go online and use a search engine to find the music you need. This is extremely helpful if you're in a rural school district.

Choosing the Best Notation Software for Your Program

Generally speaking, going to state and national music conferences gives you an opportunity to keep up with current trends in music technology. When choosing notation software, there are some basic questions you need to ask:

- Can inexperienced users use the program with a minimal amount of difficulty?
- Will it satisfy the needs of advanced users?
- Will the program allow me to extract and print individual parts?
- Does it play back multiple parts or just a single part?
- Will I be able to input dynamic and expression marks?
- Do the parts automatically line up in measures, or will I have to do it manually?
- How many parts can be saved if I'm writing or arranging a full score?
- If I'm including transposable parts, will the program automatically transpose them?
- Can I print professional-looking parts?
- Will I be able to input lyrics if needed?

The answers to those questions will be used to decide on the software cost and how much of your budget will need to be allocated. If you purchase the software while you are building your program, it is wise to purchase the software you expect to be using in your fifth year. Don't purchase something you will have to replace because your program has outgrown it.

Using Play-Along Software and Hardware

Smartmusic is not the only play-along software. There are other products that use the play-along function without giving your students a chance to record or submit to you for feedback or grading. These programs and hardware are just designed to allow your students to practice. There's software available that allows you to scan your score or their parts into your computer and have it automatically notated so that students may play along with it. Some will play the entire score with dynamics and expression markings while others will simply play the selected parts.

Some people think of play-along recordings just being used by individuals or small groups, but if you play them through your classroom audio system, your group can play along with the recordings. You can even set the device on "loop" (repeat specific sections of the piece) so that you can work on specific problem areas. This enables you to move through the ensemble to give individual assistance to students who may be having problems that need your attention. Using Smartmusic in this way enables you to have the challenging parts appear on a screen so your students can read the music as they play.

The beauty of most technologies for playing along is that they can be used together with very little effort. Smartmusic is an all-in-one package, but most notation software can be matched with play-along programs to give the same or similar benefits (Sibelius and Finale have similar components to Smartmusic).

Jazz play-along software:

Genius Jamtracks
Jammates
JJazzLab
Jazz300
SessionBand
Realbook software
iReal Pro
tomplay.com
Band in a Box
Amazing Slow Downer

PowerPoint

Having students engaged in class rather than being an audience for a lecture is valuable. PowerPoint allows you to have interactive discussions so that students are participants in the learning process, not just passive learners having information given to them. As with using tablets and smartphones, students can see the information and digest it or ask questions that will stimulate the learning process. You can combine playing and researching by including music to be played as stylistic and periodic information given on screen. Google, Evernote, and others allow multiple users to input information that can be disseminated or included in a single PowerPoint presentation. As stated earlier, Google Slides does the same things as PowerPoint.

Videotaping Your Jazz Ensemble

Just as PowerPoint is an important visual aid for teaching, videotaping your group can be a powerful tool. It combines the aural and visual elements needed for your students to evaluate their performance. As your students watch and listen to their performances and rehearsals, they will notice things that you cannot tell them to notice. Because most people are visually oriented, watching a video can be a much more valuable tool than listening alone. Guided viewing exercises are valuable, and most digital video equipment uses digital stereo sound. Zoom has a handheld device that combines digital audio recording along with high-definition video recording. Your performances are valuable recruiting tools, so make sure you only post what you and your students consider your best work.

Technology Resources on the Internet

Besides the pages listed earlier in the chapter, here are some more sites that are useful:

>https://www.smartmusic.com
>https://www.sweetwater.com/
>https://www.soundtree.com/
>https://www.ti-me.org/
>https://www.finalemusic.com/
>https://www.nafme.org/
>https://www.avid.com/sibelius
>https://www.avid.com/

Technology Resources in Book Form

Kearns, Ronald E. 2011. *Quick Reference for Band Directors*. Lanham, MD: Rowman & Littlefield.

Kearns, Ronald E. 2017. *Recording Tips for Music Educators*. New York: Oxford University Press

Rudolph, T. E. 2004. *Teaching Music with Technology*. 2nd ed. Wyncote, PA: Technology Institute for Music Educators.

Turner, Cynthia Johnston. 2013. *Another Perspective*. Reston, VA: National Association for Music Education.

11

Choosing Literature for Your Jazz Ensemble

There are several good composers for jazz ensembles and combos. JW Pepper and SheetMusicPlus are two of the leading suppliers of music from all publishers if you want to see all available music. Or you can visit each publisher's website to select from their catalogues only. Each publisher provides recordings of songs in their catalogue that you can listen to and decide which songs are best for your group. After you have selected the first songs for your first performance, it's helpful to have your students listen to songs that are available to choose for the next performance. The theory for that is that when students help select the music, it causes them to "buy into" what you're trying to achieve. It becomes "our band" rather than just being your band. It may seem like semantics, but ownership in the program causes them to work harder toward group goals.

Following are lists of some of the best publishers, composers, and arrangers for jazz ensembles.

Suggested Publishers for Jazz Ensemble

Advance Music
Alfred Music Publishing
C. L. Barnhouse

Edition Andel
Editions Marc Reift
The FJH Music Company Inc.
Hal Leonard
Heritage Music Press
Jalen Publishing
Jazz Lines Publications
JPM Music Publications
Kendor Music Publishing
Molenaar Edition
Neil A. Kjos Music Company
Queenwood Publications
Sierra Music
Southern Music Company
Twin Towers Music Publications
Walrus Music Publishing

Suggested Composers for Jazz Ensemble

Andy Clark
Bill Holman
Dean Sorenson
Doug Beach
Duke Ellington
George Gershwin
Gordon Goodwin
Harry Warren
Howard Rowe
John Edmondson
Larry Neeck
Lennie Niehaus
Les Hooper
Mike Carubia
Mike Kamuf
Mike Lewis
Neal Hefti
Paul Clark

Robert Lowden
Shelly Berg
Victor Lopez

Suggested Arrangers for Jazz Ensemble

Andy Clark
Bill Holman
Bob Curnow
Bob Florence
Dave Wolpe
Frank Mantooth
Gordon Goodwin
Jerry Nowak
John Berry
Mark Taylor
Matt Catingub
Michael Sweeney
Mike Carubia
Mike Kamuf
Mike Lewis
Mike Tomaro
Paul Murtha
Peter Blair
Roy Phillippe
Sammy Nestico
Tom Kubis
Victor Lopez

When choosing compositions or arrangements for your group, note that publishers have a grading system for the level of difficulty. It's best to look at the score and listen to the music before purchasing. There are also YouTube videos of school groups performing most of the available music; listen to them so that you can clearly hear the challenges you and your students will face.

12

Quick Repairs and Instrument Maintenance

Every jazz director has to know how to perform emergency repairs on instruments. A bridge will need to be reset, a string will break, a drum pedal will need adjustments, an amp will go out—just before the performance! Your students will panic, but you will need to know a quick fix. This chapter will give you ways to do a temporary fix for some common problems. You will need to get the instrument or piece of equipment to a licensed repair person as soon as possible after the performance.

Quick Repairs

You can be sure that "Murphy's Law" about something bad happening at the worst possible time will come true. Just as you've gotten everything done in your preparation for a performance and you are ready to take the stage, a student will bring you a broken instrument. Every broken instrument must be repaired by someone certified to do so, but just before going onstage is not the time to try to get them to fix an instrument. That means you need to be able to perform "quick fixes." A quick fix is meant to be a temporary repair to get the student through a performance, after which the instrument will need to be checked by a certified repair person as soon as possible. For some repair jobs all you will need are items found in a utility repair kit. Some of the things you'll need are not just for instrument repairs. Glue, rubber bands, string, thin wires, cigarette wrapping papers, and a host of other common materials can all be used for temporary repairs. Being able to look at the instrument and diagnose the problem is the first step.

Before you start the repair, be sure that there are no other options. If you have a backup instrument that can be used or, worse case, a backup player, make that your first option. If you don't know how well your repair will work, it's best that you not attempt it.

Following are some common problems that will need immediate attention.

Saxophones

Saxophones have so many things that can go wrong: a pad falls out, a spring dislodges, an octave key gets bent, a ligature breaks, no sound comes out when the student attempts to play, low notes won't come out. Here are some quick checks and some quick fixes.

Pad Falls Out

It's very common for temperature changes to cause a pad to become unseated and fall out. Sometimes it doesn't fall out; it just becomes unseated. If it doesn't fall out, you may have to do a simple check to locate the problem. A repair person will drop a leak light down into the instrument and check to see if light is escaping. Most band directors don't have leak lights. A flashlight can be used instead. While the student places their fingers on each key and closes them, hold the flashlight at the top of the instrument where the neck would be attached. If light is escaping, that means air is escaping. This is commonly known as a leak. The repair may not require you to remove the pad from the instrument. You may just need a butane lighter to heat the pad and make it expand. Do not let the flame hit the pad. Hold the lighter about two inches over the key and move it in a circular motion. The idea is to get the pad warm enough to expand. Periodically check with the flashlight to see if light is still escaping. Repeat the process until there is no light escaping or the student can produce an acceptable sound. If the pad has fallen out, you'll need to reseat it. You'll need the butane lighter, the flashlight, a glue stick or rubber glue, a small screwdriver, and a towel that won't leave particles on the pad.

Place the pad on a towel or paper towel face down with the back facing you. Heat the glue stick or apply rubber glue to the center of the pad. Use a very small amount because it will expand and spread. You don't want the glue to go to the edges because you'll glue the key shut! Place the pad into the key and make sure it is even with the key all around. Close the key and hold the key shut for five minutes. Do not use superglue because if you need to move the pad in any direction, superglue won't let you move it. If you need to reseat the pad using a glue stick or rubber glue, heating the key or pad will allow you to move the key. Once again, if you use superglue, the pad will not move. But if super glue is your only option, you will need to make sure that you place the pad precisely where it needs to be the first time. The other problem with superglue is that if you attempt to move the pad, part of it may detach and stick to the metal key. With a glue stick or rubber glue you can shift the key until it's set correctly. If you have used too much glue, an alcohol swab can remove the glue and enable you to repeat the process until it's correctly done. Take the instrument to a repair person as soon after the concert as possible.

Bent Octave Key

When saxophone players put the neck on the instrument, they sometimes push down and bend or dislocate the octave key. To check for the octave key functioning properly, have the student play a G using the octave key and letting it go. If either the high G or low G doesn't play, there's a problem with the octave key. If the octave mechanism is not touching the ring at the bottom of the octave key or is not pushing the octave key open, the key is bent. Repair people don't like non–repair people to attempt to bend the octave key, but an emergency repair before a performance makes it a "necessary evil"—you have no choice. Using one hand to lightly press the top of the octave key down, use your thumb to push the bottom of the key down so that the key mechanism can touch it. If the key won't open, push the bottom up but only enough so that the key will open only when the octave key is pressed (do not press hard). Hold the top of the octave key down on the seating as you bend the bottom of the key up or down. Because there is a small pad at the top of the octave key, visually check it to see if it is torn or missing. If it's torn or missing, there's nothing you can do. If it has fallen out, handle it the same way you replaced other pads that needed to be reseated.

Ligature Breaks or Is Missing

The ligature is an important part of sound production on a saxophone. The ligature holds the reed in place. Most squeaks, lack of sound production if the reed isn't cracked or broken, or the sound of air escaping are indications of a ligature problem. There are generally two screws on most ligatures. If one screw is missing, you can still get good but not ideal sound using one screw. If there is only one screw, it should be placed in the bottom hole. Have the student attempt to play and adjust the tightness to get the best possible sound. If the ligature cannot be repaired or is missing, there are some less-than-ideal solutions. Solution one involves using one or two rubber bands. Place the reed in the proper position on the mouthpiece and wrap it around the mouthpiece by doubling it. Do not break the rubber band. You don't want the reed to shift to one side or the other, so double the rubber band until the reed is secure. The reed should sit in the same position it would if it were on the mouthpiece with an actual ligature. The second solution is not ideal but works fine in an emergency. Using Scotch tape, masking tape, or a small strip of duct tape, secure the reed to the mouthpiece by wrapping the tape around the bottom of the reed. This is less than ideal because, unlike using the rubber bands, the tape will not allow you to reposition the reed unless you remove the tape and start over. With the rubber band, you can hold it in place and slide the reed up and down. Because the tape adheres to the reed and the mouthpiece, once it's set, it's set; you won't be able to move the reed. This is good if you position the reed properly because it will hold the reed in place perfectly. If you don't place the reed properly, you'll have to repeat the process until it works. After the performance you'll need to purchase a new ligature.

Springs Become Unset

The first indication of a spring problem is that a key won't close or open. The spring looks like a thick needle that is pointed at the end. It is set on a small "post" that's attached to the rod for the key. There's a groove in the rod that allows the spring to be set against it. The end of the spring fits into the indentation. Look between the rods and see if all of the springs are set in the indentation. If one is not making contact with the groove, you'll need to reset it. Depending on the location and size of your finger, you can push the spring back in place. If it's a small space, a pencil tip or eraser can guide the spring back in place. If needed, a small screwdriver (like the ones used for eyeglasses) can be used. Simply push the middle of the spring until you bend the spring enough to get it to seat correctly. You can use anything that is small enough to fit between the rods to push the spring in place. The object is to delicately set the spring into the groove. Have the student press the key to see if it goes back in place. If it does the spring is set correctly. If the spring breaks or comes out, your only option is to have a repair person replace it.

Trumpets

There are a few problems with trumpets that are rather common. A mouthpiece will get stuck, a pad will fall out of the spit key, valves will be stuck or sluggish coming back up, slides will get stuck. Because there are fewer moving parts than there are on saxophones, there are fewer problems. That doesn't mean that you won't have to do emergency repairs; it just means there are fewer things to check.

Every band room has to have at least one mouthpiece puller. The puller is designed to give equal pressure on all sides so that you can twist and pull out the mouthpiece without damaging the shaft. There was a time when band directors would put the mouthpiece between door hinges and pull until the mouthpiece came out. This usually resulted in damage to the instrument and the door! The mouthpiece puller performs a difficult task in a short amount of time. Do not fall into the idea that anything you can clamp the mouthpiece to will pull the mouthpiece out. You will do substantial damage to the instrument.

Just like with saxophones, a missing pad on a trumpet causes a leak and prevents sound production. A fuzzy sound or no sound indicates that you need to check spit keys or spit valves. Open the spit key/valve and visually inspect the pad. If the pad is not seated correctly, you'll need to do what you did with saxophone pads. Because these pads are smaller, the repair will be more tedious. You may need to have tweezers to hold and seat the pad depending on the size of your fingers. To apply the glue to the key, you can use a Q-tip or small swab to put a small amount of glue to the seating of the key. Once again, too much glue being used will spread and glue the key shut. Hold the key closed for five minutes by lightly pressing it. Have the student play a long tone and listen to the sound. If it's fuzzy or you hear air escaping, you'll need to reseat the pad. Students sometimes bend or break the spit key spring, so check that also, once you have checked the pad.

The most common problem for trumpets is with the valves. There are many different problems that valves have. Some can be fixed with a quick fix, and others have to be repaired by a repair person. Visually inspect the problem valve. If the top of the valve is bent, there is no quick fix you can perform. If the valve is not bent, your first check should be to twist the top of the valve until you hear it lock in place. This makes sure the valve is in the correct position for the air to pass through for tone production. If there's still no sound, unscrew and remove the valve from its seating (tube). Check the spring to make sure that when the valve is depressed, the spring will push it back up. Place the spring back inside the seating and use a towel to clean the valve. Warm soapy water will work but there are products made specifically for cleaning valves.

Sometimes the problem is as simple as "gunk" buildup preventing the valve to set in the proper place. A buildup of gunk will slow or obstruct the smooth movement of the valve. Anything that obstructs valve movement or airflow will affect sound production.

Take each valve out and clean with warm, soapy water to make sure gunk is not affecting valve movement. There are valve brushes that will scrape the gunk away. If each spring is good and each valve is clean, things should work properly. Because students sometimes remove valves and put them back into the wrong valve space, check the numbers on the valves to make sure they are in the right place.

Trombones

The most common problems for trombone are stuck mouthpieces, stuck or sticky slides, and spit key problems. Use the mouthpiece puller for a stuck mouthpiece as described for trumpet. For stuck slides, clean the slide with warm soapy water, oil the slide with slide oil, and check its movement. The procedure for the spit valve is exactly the same as the trumpet. Of all of the instruments, the trombone is the least difficult to fix. Dents, bent slides, and gunk on the slide are the most serious problems. You can clean the gunk off, but dents require a certified repair person.

Amplifiers

Electronic equipment is difficult to repair and in most cases requires a professional repair person. If you have vintage equipment that uses tubes, the most common problem is a blown tube. You can easily replace the tubes, and it's recommended that you keep spare tubes handy. Most amps now use transistors and circuit boards and require precision repairs. The most common problems are with knobs and cords. A knob will come off, and wires will fray or break. Because of the possibility of fire or shorting out your electricity, don't attempt quick-fix repairs.

Guitar and Electric Bass

There are several problems that guitars and electric basses have in common. The biggest problem is broken strings. Before every performance you should be sure to have six guitar strings and four bass strings so that you can replace a broken string. The most common reason for strings breaking is overtightening while tuning. String replacement is not difficult, but it is tedious. Check the unbroken strings to see how the strings need to be strung. Make sure you get the string in the right place at the bottom. Pull it tight and make sure it locks in place. Next, put it through the tuning peg/key and tighten it. The best way to get the string in place is to alternate tightening and loosening so that the string stretches. The stretching assures that once you tighten the string, it won't loosen and lose pitch while playing. The more serious issue for guitars and basses is tuning keys. Depending on the mechanism, keys sometimes won't hold in place. Less expensive instruments don't have grooves on the tuning mechanism and will not lock into place. There's very little you can do in that case. Other problems involve the pickup. A pickup problem cannot be repaired through a quick fix.

Double Bass

The upright string double bass has many problems that can come up. The most common problem is a bridge falling out or breaking, a sound post issue, broken strings, and cracks in the body.

The bridge falling out of place or breaking usually happens when basses are moved from place to place. If the bridge falls out, you can put it back in place by loosening the strings and putting the bridge against the body. Put each string in the grooves on the bass and tighten them. Without tightening completely, use your fingers to push the bridge firmly in place. Be sure that the bridge is firmly in place against the body of the bass and adjust it slightly to the position that is most comfortable for the player.

The next common problem is the sound post falling. On a full-sized bass, you may be able to use a wire hanger to retrieve the sound post from the inside bottom of the bass by going inside the F hole in the center of the bass. If you can retrieve it, you will need to use your hands to put it back in place. Even if you can put it back in place, this is at best a temporary fix, and a certified repair person will need to make the proper placement and adjustments.

The most important thing about quick repairs is that after you make a quick repair, you take the instrument to a certified repair shop. You may or may not have made a long-term repair, but if you don't get it checked out, you may find yourself in the same position again. There's no way to predict if your repair is a long-term fix, but a repair person can inspect your work.

13

Developing a Support Group for Your Jazz Ensemble

If you're developing a jazz program in a school where you have a band program, chances are you have a band boosters group in place. All you will need to do for your jazz ensemble is customize your current support system to include jazz parents or develop a separate group. In some cases an "instrumental" parent support group will suffice as long as it meets the needs of band, jazz, and orchestra students. This chapter offers some practical advice on developing a jazz parent group that can stand alone or be incorporated into an existing parent group. The National Association for Music Education (NAfME) has a *Music Booster Manual* that outlines its policies on music boosters and music teachers' responsibilities. This is a helpful resource whether or not you are a member of NAfME.

Establishing a New Parent Group

The most important first step in developing a parent support group is deciding on the group's purpose and how it will function. Will the group be a pool for chaperones or a solid base for fundraising and other activities? Deciding this will determine what kind of leadership team you will have in place and how much oversight will be required of you. You don't want your parent group to go out on their own and do things that will not positively affect your jazz program. Unfortunately, the "tail wagging the dog" sinks a lot of programs. Once parent groups go out on their own, it's difficult to reel them back in.

One of the first steps in forming the group is to establish the leadership structure. The smaller the leadership group, the more effective it will be. Each member of the leadership team should have a specific function and purpose. You will need a chairperson who will coordinate all activities of the parent group along with you. This individual should be someone who can influence others into action, knows the community and your program goals, knows how to organize projects, and can work well with others. It should be clear that the parent group cannot do anything without your approval and that their function is to assist you in furthering the advancement of jazz activities in your school. Since you will have a mission statement in place and your philosophy of music education is clearly stated, all activities of the boosters' group should support the mission. The next member of the leadership team should be the financial officer. This person is responsible for keeping a record of all funds brought into the program and maintaining an accurate account of all expenditures. They will be the liaison between you, the school administration, and the school district. The financial officer should be someone who can keep accurate records and can be bonded if that's a requirement of your school district. It is your responsibility to explain to the financial officer the school's policies governing fundraising, budget development, and purchase requirements (bid lists, etc.) This officer should not be the only person who can sign checks or have access to funds. Your signature should be required along with one other person on checks. This makes sure that no expenditure can be made without your approval. The booster group should not be responsible for purchases that are the responsibility of the school or school district. Every school has a business manager or financial secretary who handles all school purchases, purchase orders, and requisitions (principals in smaller schools handle all finances). Once the boosters' financial person is selected, the two of you should meet with the business manager or financial secretary and/or principal to go over all of the school's and school district's financial policies.

The third member of the leadership team should be the activity coordinator. This person is responsible for overseeing all of the committees you'll need. There will be fundraising activities, travel activities, chaperone needs, and uniform/wardrobe maintenance/purchase, among others. Various members of the booster group will be in charge of these activities and will have others working with them. The activity coordinator will help make sure your "people resources" are not spread too thin. They will also make sure that two or more committees can work together.

Leadership Function

Once your three leaders have been put in place, you will need to decide on exactly what support you will need. The problem some directors have with forming a support group is not clearly defining needs, roles, and responsibilities. These roles and responsibilities should be outlined and assigned to specific people and/or committees. These individuals and committees should have specific guidelines and must be able to work closely with you as jazz ensemble director. As the director, you will have many responsibilities, and the booster group should not create extra work for you. Ideally, this group and its committees should be in place to assist you in developing a successful jazz program. You should not micromanage; take advantage of the expertise of those you have selected and those who volunteer for committees.

The establishment of rules and guidelines (bylaws) is important. These rules and bylaws should clearly state the purpose and function of the group and their administrative limitations. It's imperative that the group knows that it must abide by school and district policies and cannot make decisions concerning your group without your approval.

The following is a sample of booster group bylaws:

The _____ Jazz Boosters Organization is established to offer support to the _____ jazz ensemble. The function of the group is to provide financial and emotional support, chaperones, support activities, awards and recognition, and other tasks requested by the jazz ensemble director. A checking account will be established and two signatures will be required to conduct any business or write/endorse any checks. One of those signatures must always be the jazz director's. No business or official meetings may be held without the jazz director's knowledge or presence. This does not include committee meetings as directed by the director or Jazz Boosters Organization.

These bylaws should be consistent with your school's policies and must be approved by your school's administration. Since as band director you may have an existing band boosters group, you can also make it an instrumental boosters group and have committees specific to band, jazz, or orchestra needs. If it is a joint group, take into consideration how financial needs and account setups may vary. Have each group keep accurate records of all funds. If your groups take trips together, there should be a combined bank account for trip payments and fundraisers. The band, jazz, and orchestra committees should keep accurate records of all funds that are specific for band, jazz, or orchestra. It is recommended that three separate accounts be maintained and that you have a special "trip" (travel) account for each group. This is especially important if students will benefit from funds they raise during fundraising activities. Trip accounting is best done by maintaining records for individual students. This way, when trip payments are tallied, you can figure in any percentages from fundraising that are credited to individual students (via spreadsheets). Some parents don't like students other than their own benefiting from their hard work. It helps that at the beginning of each fundraiser, it's clear what percentage of the fundraiser benefits the group as a whole and what percentage will benefit individual students. You can include a statement to that effect in your bylaws.

Forming Committees

Most school districts have a Back-to-School night or a first-of-the-year Parents/Teachers meeting. This will be your first time meeting your students' parents. When you meet with the parents, it's good to have an agenda to outline what you and your group hope to achieve. Your music education philosophy, a proposed mission statement, your handbook, and a syllabus will help make it clear what you hope to achieve. Having an agenda speaks to your organizational skills and that you value your parents' time.

At this meeting, have parents fill out cards with their name and contact information (email, phone numbers, name and address). You should also have a list of your expected needs so that they can select activities they can assist you with (match the parents' skill inventory with your needs list). If you know fundraising activities you plan to have, you can be specific; if not, you can ask for parents to sign up for a general fundraising committee. You will need chaperones for local and out-of-town trips, uniforms or special attire purchases/maintenance, equipment purchases and maintenance, and so on. This will be your first chance to organize your boosters; make the most of it.

Another important committee formed at the beginning of building your program will be a publicity/social media committee. Publicity directly affects recruiting and helps keep your program from being one of the best-kept secrets of your school. If you or your students have accomplished something that deserves wider recognition, this committee should prepare and disseminate information on social media and to local news organizations. Posting pictures of performances, highlighting student achievements and successes, and announcing performances are also very important functions of a publicity committee. As director, you'll have your hands full of music-related items, and making posters or posting on social media will take time away from performance preparation. You must be willing to sell your program, and "advertising" is a very important part. Have your school's newspaper, web page, and all of its social media pages carry information of your program's successes and upcoming events. Have a parent or group of students specifically tasked with posting information about your group every week.

A lot of programs fail because parents aren't engaged and give assistance. Take an inventory of skills from your parents to find out what they can do to help your program and help defray program costs. For example, if you have tailors or seamstresses in your parent's group, they may be able to make outfits for performances. Buying material is a lot less expensive than having to buy full outfits. You may just need accessories made rather than full outfits.

Social Media

Sometimes band is the best-kept secret in a school. The same is true for jazz ensembles. Your most important tool for recruiting and retaining is good publicity. There should never be anything positive that happens in your program that isn't shared with your school community. A subcommittee of your parent group should be dedicated to publicity. The subcommittee should maintain your social media pages, submit information to your school's social media pages, and communicate with the school community through any media outlet the school has. Word of mouth even through social media will build your program and encourage your students. Using posters in your classroom or on school walls to recognize group or individual achievements is very important for communicating your successes. The overall morale of your students will increase when they realize that they are valued. Students tend to join and stay in activities and programs where they feel they are appreciated and valued. Your parents can help immensely. They will play a major part in preparing for and implementing trips and festivals that will help your program grow, the subject of the next chapter.

14

Trips and Festivals

One of the ways to make your program grow is to participate in festivals and assessments for your students to learn from adjudicators how they measure up to acceptable performance standards. At assessments and festivals there are adjudicators/judges who listen to your students' performance and evaluate them on standards that include the quality of their performance, stage appearance, adherence to the score, overall interpretation, and many other factors that contribute to an acceptable performance. Besides preparing for the performance you will be planning trip logistics and other details that can be overwhelming. There are festival companies that will assist you in your trip planning, travel, lodging, and fun activities that will help you and your students get the most out of your experience. As was mentioned in the previous chapter, you will need help from your parent boosters to make sure that everything is planned in detail. Students will need to be assigned rooms, meals must be planned that will require meeting special diet plans for individual students, instruments must be transported, and many other minute details must be covered. This chapter is intended to give you a blueprint for trip planning and implementation.

How Do You Decide What Festivals and Assessments to Participate In?

As you're deciding on what festivals to attend, you must first decide on the performance level of your group. Are you going to be evaluated on your performance through comments only, or are you going to compete with other groups? Most school systems have local assessments for bands, orchestras, and jazz ensembles. These festivals are designed to be noncompetitive only, and your group is judged by a specified standard. These standards have rankings for Superior, Excellent, Good, Fair, and Poor. It's important that you review the standards and the evaluation criteria with your students. Remind your students that the judges are only hearing a snapshot of their performance abilities and don't know how far the students have progressed in learning and performing their pieces. The judges are objectively listening to the performance with scores in front of them so that they can assess the performance based on established standards. Are the students following score instructions, are they being accurate with their interpretation, are they keeping a steady tempo, are they following articulation markings and playing correct rhythms? Before your students perform in front of judges, you should take them through the score sheet and evaluate whether they are meeting performance standards. The best way to evaluate student performances is to record your group's rehearsals and use guided listening to help students hear what you hear. This bears repeating: if you decide that they are ready, then decide if you're going to participate for comments only or for one of the five ratings.

Comments only is generally the best choice for newly established groups. Judges give comments that will help you and your students improve on or polish your performance. They generally are focused on how you can improve on your performance and offer feedback to how well you met the standards or what you need to do to meet the standards.

Trip Logistics

When preparing for a trip there are many logistics that need to be taken care of. First, you need to make sure that the cost of the trip is not prohibitive for students who can't afford to pay for the trip. Since you need all parts covered for a good performance, you can't afford to leave any players behind. You will need to secure funds to cover students who may need financial assistance. There are several ways to do this. Some schools and school districts have funds set aside to help students with travel costs. These funds are set aside specifically to make sure that all students have access to educational experiences. Title One schools have special funds for underprivileged students, but other schools have similar funds set aside for students who may have financial difficulties. You can also have fundraising activities that allow students to raise funds for their own personal accounts to pay for their trip. Your parent boosters can structure your fundraising in such a way that it defrays the overall cost of the trip and allows students to raise money for themselves to apply toward the costs. Your student handbook should give a complete description of how you will make trips and activities accessible for all students in your program.

Parent permission for in-district and out-of-district trips is important. Besides giving permission for their child to travel with you, parents will need to provide a medical form that spells out any conditions or special needs for their child. This includes food allergies, special dietary needs, and permission to provide lifesaving care in case the parents can't immediately be reached and to deal with any other medical issues that may arise during the trip. Emergencies will pop up, and your advanced planning can help prevent a bad or life-threatening situation. If your group separates from you and students are with your chaperones, each chaperone needs to have the students' medical forms with them. Once again, advanced planning is vital.

One of your chaperones will need to be in charge of making sure your students have their music, their instruments and accessories, their outfits, and anything else they need for the performance. Many band directors have stories about stepping onstage and discovering students are missing something that is vital for their performance. Onstage is the last place you want to make that discovery. You need to develop an in-depth itinerary that spells out times and expectations for the students. Every chaperone needs specific responsibilities that will relieve you from being overwhelmed by logistics that aren't part of your performance schedule. You should not be trying to find a mouthpiece or a missing folder before the performance. Advance planning will enable you to focus on the music side of the performance rather than the mundane items that lead up to the stage performance. Be clear: you are responsible for everything but that doesn't mean that you have to do everything. Delegate responsibilities to other adults with you.

Festival Performance Etiquette

Don't assume your students know what proper performance etiquette is. Remind them that there should be no talking or moving onstage prior to or during the performance. Gum chewing should not be permitted. Students should be taught how to tap their heels lightly or their toes inside their shoes without lifting their foot off the floor. Foot tapping is a distraction and, worse, can cause rushing. Many recordings of school groups are ruined by foot tapping picked up by microphones.

Establish the level of your students' stands so that they can look above the top of them to see the conductor (a lot of groups use band fronts, which are lower than stands). Decide whether students will sit on the edge of their seats or sit with their backs on their chairs. This decision affects the uniformity, so it's not a petty decision. Performance etiquette impacts your overall performance, so plan everything carefully. Adjudicators form an impression of your group from the way they carry themselves going on and off the stage. You don't want anything to detract from your performance.

The way your students carry their instruments to and from the stage is not just about the visuals, it's very practical. You don't want your students carrying their instruments in such a way that they can be bumped or hit. Bridges have been broken or knocked out of position by a simple bump or knock, reeds get broken, mouthpieces get jammed. Don't let your students carry their instruments in such a way that they can hit another student, stand, chair, or wall.

Trip Planning Checklist

Before planning any out-of-district trips, you should consult your principal or music supervisor to determine school and district travel policies. When securing buses for out-of-town trips, you will need to make a deposit. These deposits are usually nonrefundable. You don't want to make a deposit and then find out that you can't go on the trip! Be sure to get all necessary approvals before planning or announcing the trip. Once you secure all approvals, then you may start putting in place all of your logistics. Here's a sample timeline:

1. Secure approval for your trips during the summer before school starts.
2. Survey for parents who are in health care. With or without a health-care worker, you will need the medical forms mentioned earlier.
3. Encourage parents of students who require medications or special services to travel with you. Food allergies, religious diets, and other special needs should be addressed.

International Festivals and Trips

Planning an international trip is quite often a two-year endeavor. Because of finances, a need for passports, security, health and medical concerns, air travel, itinerary setup, and supervision require a lot of planning. There are international tour companies that can provide you with a list of needs and things that you need to do before you leave. Except for the need for passports, visas, and special needs for foreign travel, planning an international trip is basically the same as planning for an out-of-state trip. Travel agencies will handle securing airline tickets, lodging, performance venues, festival sites, and itineraries for you. Most educational travel companies are associated with international festivals and will build your itinerary around festival performances. They are also aware of fees and costs that you may not be aware of. They help with things like baggage weight requirements and other things related to international air travel. Chaperone requirements for foreign travel may be different from domestic travel, and the travel company will walk you through the requirements.

Most school districts require you to furnish them with a complete itinerary and the educational benefits of the trip. You, your school, and your school district can be held liable for anything that happens to your students on an international trip, so once again, planning is vital. Travel plans and details should be spelled out in detail. All of the things previously mentioned should be included in your itinerary and travel plans.

As you plan for health care, don't forget that dental care is part of health care. Dental care in most foreign countries may be different from here, but the American embassy or consulate there can provide you with a list of either dental professionals that serve the consulate/embassy or dentists in the host country who can help (the tour company can also help with this).

You should secure passports at least ten months before your trip. You don't want to risk students not being able to get passports or visas, so start early and have students and chaperones show you their passports. You may not be able to take larger instruments with you, so ask your travel company to assist you with securing instruments. If you have enough students to charter a flight, you may be able to carry large instruments and equipment with you. Make sure that you have adapters for foreign electrical outlets. Contact the State Department to find out about any special requirements for large groups in your host country. Because of the COVID pandemic, a lot of countries have special rules in place that you may not be aware of that will have an impact on your travel inside the host country.

Before you meet with parents to discuss local, out-of-state, or international trips and festivals, make sure you have the answers to frequently asked questions. Once again, educational travel companies have many of the answers you will need. Contact them and tell them what you want to do, and they will be able to guide you through the process. Do not try to do this alone; travel companies know exactly what you need to do, and they are there to assist you.

15

Recording Your Group during Rehearsals

A lot of this chapter has been mentioned in previous chapters, but this chapter goes into greater detail. Recording your group during rehearsals is an important way to get your students to hear themselves and understand that you are not telling them that there are problems just to fill the class period. While they are playing, they can't always focus on what the group sounds like as a whole. Having a focused listening session during the rehearsal gives them the opportunity to hear what they as a group sound like. It's interesting how well they will recognize mistakes and items that need improvement once they have an "out-of-band" experience. During guided listening you can help them hear things from your perspective, and they will discover that there are things that need to be fixed.

When conducting guided listening, it's important that you play the recording without commenting. If you give them an adjudication form to follow, they can grade their performance and make comments that will be helpful for the group. You'll be surprised by how astute your students are and how much they hear when you play back their performance. Don't allow the students to make generalized comments without offering ways to improve the things they are criticizing. Do not allow the critiques to become personal. As described in an earlier chapter, even though there is one person per part in some cases and everyone knows who is being described, it's important to refer to the part and not the person. This is a team-building exercise and you don't want anyone to "check out" during the process. After you play the recording and your students have given their feedback, it's your job to pull things together. It's important that you point out how valuable their observations and input are to improving the quality of the group's performance. You may not have much to add if you've guided the listening in the direction that will help your students hear what you hear in the recording.

Student-Directed Warmups

When preparing to record your group, you can have students conduct the warmup. Having students stand in front of the band to direct the warmup helps them hear things from your perspective. They are not aware of how different things sound when they're playing inside the band and how they sound in front of the band. This is very similar to how they will hear things during the guided listening activity. Instead of focusing on their part or their section, standing in front of the band helps them hear the importance of balance, intonation, and attacks and releases. Those three things are important for a good group performance. As you set up the microphones, you'll want to capture the entire group and soloists. Following are descriptions of microphone placement and the importance of microphone proximity.

Microphone Setup and Placement

As previously stated, some people think that recording is as simple as placing microphones in front of the group and hitting "Record." Recording your group requires planning, proper microphone placement, proximity of microphones, direction of the microphone, and the kinds of microphones needed. Generally, the fewer microphones used, the better the recording. You may or may not need a mixing board to capture the best audio for your group. Because jazz ensembles are smaller than other groups, you will need to record the overall sound, soloists, piano, upright bass, and drum set. You may or may not want to run the guitar, electric piano, and upright bass or electric bass through the soundboard. Sometimes you may want to run the electric instruments through a soundboard to get a good balance so that you can record the group sound without having to do a postrecording mixing session.

Common Setups for Microphones

The concept of recording is based on capturing audio on a recording the same way the ears perceive sound. Since your ears are about seven and a half inches apart, the best microphone setup is a parallel pair of matching microphones also set seven and a half inches apart. Using a fifteen-foot microphone stand at a center point of the rehearsal room or performance area works for most groups.

The simplest way to discover the best placement for the parallel pair of microphones is to walk around the room clapping to find the "sweet spot." The sweet spot is the place in the room where you don't hear more sound or echo coming from the left or right. You will hear the sound centered. That's where you place the microphones. If you have soloists, you have two options. One is to place a solo microphone in front of the rhythm section and have soloists walk over and play there. The microphone can be turned off until the soloist stands in front of it. Another option is to place a solo microphone in front of each section and have the soloists play toward the microphone or move to a position in front of the microphone. For group balance the microphone should not be on until the soloist needs it. Some groups use an overhead boom microphone in smaller spaces. This setup requires the group to be balanced because you won't have the opportunity to add balance in postrecording mixing.

There is another option for a matching pair of microphones that is an X pattern or a Y pattern. The X pattern (ninety-degree spacing) is a pattern where you place microphones on top of each other, forming an X. The microphone on the right records sound from the left, and the left microphone records sound from the right. The distance between the microphone ends should still be inches apart. The Y configuration (near-coincident matching pair) is simply taking the parallel pair and pointing them at a diagonal, left microphone pointing left and right microphone pointing right. Both the X and Y cover the largest distance from the sound source (the band).

It's important to know the difference between microphone placement and proximity. Placement refers to the overall position of the microphone and microphone stands, and proximity refers to the precise location (nearness). You can have a microphone in the right spot but slightly off axis (not near enough to collect the most or strongest sound). Generally, the proximity that's best for saxophones is having very little space between the microphone and the instrument. For brasses and drums you want to have space between the microphone and the instrument so that you don't experience sound cancellation. This happens when the microphone is overloaded by the output of the instrument. Some of the most important things to consider in your recording space are the physical characteristics of the recording space. How will the size of the room affect reverberation (echo), how "live" is the space (tile floors, cinder block walls, carpet floors, wood floors, etc.)? In order to get a good recording in the circumstances just mentioned you'll need to use the clapping exercise, walking around the room to determine how loud or "live" the room is naturally. The idea of the recording is to capture what your ears hear live. When you play back the recording, each listener should hear what they heard live.

When purchasing microphones there are three basic types that should be used: omnidirectional (omni), figure of eight (multidirectional), and cardioid (directional). The idea is to collect as much sound from the sound source as possible. You will need to experiment with your group output, the room size, and its construction (cinder block, wood, etc.). There's a more advanced technique used called mid-side. Mid-side uses a matching pair facing each other or an unmatched pair touching each other. There will be a null point (position where no sound is recorded from the audience or other places you don't want to collect sound, like echoes).

The idea of this chapter is not to train you as a recording engineer but to give you a working knowledge of the recording process so that you can get a quality recording for your and your students' review. As stated previously, *Recording Tips for Music Educators* by Ronald E. Kearns (Oxford University Press) is a recommended source for more recording information.

Appendix

Permission Slip (Local)

Student's name _____

Activity _____

Activity date and time _____
(periods/classes missed)

I give _____ permission to ride school-provided transportation to _____ with the jazz ensemble on _____ (date)

I do not give _____ permission to participate in this activity. I realize this is a graded activity and my child will be penalized for not participating.

I give _____ permission to participate, but I will transport them to and from the activity.

I give _____ permission to participate in the above-named activity and to go in parent/adult-driven transportation.

Signed _____ Date _____

Permission Slip for an Out-of-Town Trip

Student's Name _____

Activity Name and Date _____

Parent's Name _____

Parent's Phone _____

I give _____ permission to travel out of town with the jazz ensemble.

Signed _____ Date _____

Glossary

A section: The first section of a tune, typically eight bars. Jazz term for the main theme.

AABA: The most common form in pop music. Most often referred to as "song form."

Alteration: The raising or lowering of a tone by a half-step from its diatonic value in a chord. Any interval may be augmented or diminished.

Altered scale: The term used for the arrangement of scale tones from a diatonic scale that changes the position of whole-steps and half-steps. Half-steps are no longer between steps 3 and 4 or 7 and 8.

Augmented: Raised by a half-step.

Augmented seventh (+7): A dominant seventh chord with a raised fifth added. The name is misleading because it is not the seventh that is augmented.

Axe: Jazz term for a jazz musician's instrument. Also used to describe the voice.

B section: The second section in AABA form. Same as the bridge.

Backbeat: Beats 2 and 4 in 4/4 time, particularly when they are strongly accented.

Ballad: A slow tune, generally a love song, filled with emotion. Ballad playing is replete with its own idiomatic devices.

Bebop: The style of jazz developed by young players in the early 1940s, particularly Charlie Parker, Dizzy Gillespie, Kenny Clarke, Charlie Christian, and Bud Powell. Characterized by rapid, many-noted improvisations using long, irregular, syncopated phrasing. Improv was based on chordal harmony rather than the tune. Alterations were used more freely than in Swing music, especially the flatted fifth and augmented eleventh. The ground beat was moved from the bass drum to the ride cymbal and the bass, and the rhythmic feel is more flowing and subtle. Instrumental virtuosity was stressed.

Block chords: A style of piano playing with both hands "locked" together, playing chords in parallel with the melody, usually in fairly close position. Also called locked hands.

Blow: The Jazz term for improvise. Sometimes called "taking a ride." Also, simply to play an instrument.

Blowing changes: Playing over chord progressions.

Blues: (1) A form normally consisting of twelve bars, staying in one key and moving to the IV chord at bar 5; (2) a melodic style, with typical associated harmonies, using certain "blues scales," riffs, and grace notes; (3) a musical genre, ancestral to jazz and part of it; (4) a feeling that is said to inform all jazz.

Boogie (boogie-woogie): A style of piano playing very popular in the 1930s. Blues, with continuous repeated eighth-note patterns in the left hand and exciting blues riffs and figures in the right hand.

Break: A transitional passage in which a soloist plays unaccompanied.

Bridge: The contrasting middle section of a tune, especially the "B" section of an AABA song form. A development section of a song in song form.

Broken time: A way of playing in which the beat is not stated explicitly. Irregular, improvised syncopation. Especially applied to bass and drum playing. Rubato playing.

Cadence: A key-establishing chord progression, generally following the circle of fifths. A turnaround is one example of a cadence. Sometimes a whole section of a tune can be an extended cadence. In understanding the harmonic structure of a tune, it's important to see which chords are connected to which others in cadences. Generally, the ii-V-I progression.

Changes: Term for chord progressions.

Channel: Another term for the bridge.

Chart: (1) Any musical score; (2) a special type of score, used by jazz musicians. Only the melody line, words (if any), and chord symbols are given. Also see "Lead sheet."

Chase: Term for trading twos, fours, and eights between two improvisers.

Chops: Technical ability to execute music physically and to negotiate chord changes. Embouchure. Also used to describe virtuosity.

Chord: The harmony at a given moment, a group of three or more notes played together(1, 3, 5). A chord is the basic unit of harmony, regarded as having a given root and specifying some other tones at certain intervals from the root, without regard to the actual voicing of the notes on the piano.

Chord tones: The root, third, fifth, and seventh of a chord (can be expanded to include the 9, 11, and 13).

Chorus: One complete cycle of a tune, one time through from top to bottom. AABA or blues form.

Chromatic: Pertaining to or derived from the chromatic scale, which includes all twelve tones to the octave. Each note is a half-step away from the next note ascending or descending.

Circle of fifths: Diagram depicting the relationship among the twelve tones of the chromatic scale, their corresponding key signatures, and the associated major and minor keys. Inverted known as the circle of fourths.

Coda: (1) A portion of a tune which seems like an ending, or extra measures, added to the last A section. It is repeated for every chorus, however. (2) An ending for a tune, used only once after the final chorus. Most often used on the "out-chorus only."

Cool: The style of the early 1950s, popularized by Miles Davis. The basis was bebop, but the fastest tempos were not used, and the sound was quiet and understated.

Counting off: Giving the tempo and meter by counting aloud or tapping the tempo.

Diatonic: An eight-tone scale.

Dig: An expression of approval.

Diminished: Lowered by a half-step (shortening the distance of an interval). A minor chord or fourth or fifth interval lowered a half-step.

Diminished scale: A scale of eight notes to the octave in alternating whole-steps and half-steps. There are just three different diminished scales. Most diminished scales contain a diminished fifth and a diminished seventh.

Diminished seventh (7): Chord composed of four notes stacked in minor thirds. The symbol is a small raised circle. If the chord tones and extensions are put together within an octave, the diminished scale results. Often called just "diminished" with "seventh" being implied.

Diminished triad: Triad composed of two stacked minor thirds; root, minor third, and diminished fifth.

Dorian mode: A scale starting on the second degree of the diatonic scale. The basis for building a chord on the ii in the ii-V-I turnaround.

Double time: A tempo twice as fast, with the time feel, bar lines, and chords moving at twice the speed.

Double time feel: A time feel twice as fast, so that written eighth notes now sound like quarter notes, while the chords continue at the same speed as before.

Eight to the bar: Continuous eighth-note rhythm, as in boogie-woogie left-hand patterns.

Extensions: The ninth, eleventh, and thirteenth of a chord.

Fake book: A collection of jazz charts, published without paying royalties and thus illegal (not in the public domain.)

Free Jazz: A style of the early and middle 1960s, involving "free" playing and an outside-of-chords effect. Atonal or multitonal.

Fusion: A style developed in the late 1960s by Wayne Shorter, Herbie Hancock, Miles Davis, Chick Corea, and others, partly as a reaction to the eclipse of jazz on the music scene by rock. Pop, rock, and funk are incorporated into jazz.

Front line: The horn players in a combo; instruments that aren't in the rhythm section.

Go out: Take the final chorus, end. Out chorus ending the song.

Grand staff: The treble and bass staves together.

Groove: An infectious feeling in the rhythm, of being perfectly centered. The rhythm section forms a recurring "pocket" for the front line to play on top of.

Ground beat: The basic metric beat, most often in quarter notes, whether explicitly stated or not.

Half-diminished (Ø): The chord with a minor third, a diminished fifth, and a minor seventh. Formally called minor seven flat five. The symbol is a small O with a diagonal slash. It is most often the harmony of the ii in a ii-V-I progression in a minor key. Two different scales have been commonly used for this chord; one with a flat ninth, the "Locrian," and one with an unflatted ninth.

Half time: A tempo half as fast.

Half time feel: A time feel half as fast, while the chords go by in the same amount of time.

Hard bop: The style of the late 1950s, engineered by Horace Silver, Art Blakey, and others. Still essentially bebop, the style used a hard-driving rhythmic feel and biting lines and harmony with urban blues, rhythm and blues, and gospel.

Harmonic rhythm: The structural organization of chord progressions in time; the rate at which the chords pass by. Since this may not be related to the rhythms of the actual notes, it is an abstract concept.

Head: The first (and last) chorus of a tune, in which the song or melody is stated without improvisation or with minimal improvisation.

Horn: A wind instrument; or any instrument. See "Axe."

Improvisation (Improv): The process of spontaneous composition over the continuously repeating cycle of chord changes of a tune. The improviser may depend on the contours of the original tune, solely on the possibilities of the chords' harmonies, or on a basis of pure melody. The "improv" also refers to the improvisational section of the tune, as opposed to the head.

Inner voice: A melodic line, no matter how fragmentary, lying between the bass and the melody. Also chord tones found within chords.

Interlude: An additional section in a tune, especially one between one person's solo and another's.

Intro (Introduction): A composed section at the beginning of a tune, heard only once.

Inversion: (1) In traditional music theory, a chord with a note other than the root in the bass; (2) with regard to any particular voicing, especially a left-hand rootless voicing, a rearrangement of the voicing by moving the bottom note up an octave.

Jazz standard: A well-known tune by a jazz musician.

Jump: A very fast 4/4, usually in a dance-band context. From the Swing period.

Latin: (1) Afro-Cuban, Brazilian, or other South American–derived. Also "straight-eight." The feel of bossa novas and sambas.

Lay out: Do not play.

Lead sheet: A form of music notation that specifies the melody and harmony (and sometimes the lyric) of a tune. See "Chart."

Left-hand rootless voicing (LHRV): A close-position voicing without a root, played mainly in the octave of middle C. The mainstream style of left-hand playing.

Line: (1) A melody of successive, single notes; (2) a composed melody over predetermined chord changes; (3) one of the different voices, such as the bass or the melody.

Lineup: The personnel of a band.

Long meter: A chart in 4/4 time is said to be written in long meter when a written eighth note feels like a quarter note, and a written half measure feels like a whole measure. In this way, for example, a sixty-four-bar tune can be written as if it were a thirty-two-bar tune, which may make it easier to read. The term, though useful, is little known.

Lydian: A major scale or chord with a raised fourth; the mode of the major scale diatonic scale built on the fourth degree of a diatonic scale. Regarded by some as the most fundamental jazz scale.

Lydian dominant: A dominant seventh scale with a raised fourth (eleventh). One of the fundamental forms of the dominant chord; also sometimes called "Lydo-Mixian." The scale/

chord most appropriate for non-V dominants, such as II7 or bVII7.

Mainstream: The style of jazz regarded by the average player as today's norm, as opposed to fusion, rock, avant-garde, and so on; sometimes the term implies a somewhat conservative, relatively diatonic vocabulary. Mainstream jazz still rests on a basis of bebop, which is why "modern" jazz is considered to have started with bebop in the early 1940s.

Medium: One of the standard jazz tempos, neither fast nor slow.

Melodic minor: In jazz, a scale with a minor third but a major sixth and seventh (both up and down). This scale and its modes (altered, half-diminished, and Lydian dominant are the familiar ones) make up a realm called melodic minor harmony. Also called "tonic minor."

Melody: Specifically, the topmost line or voice.

Meter: The organization of the beats of time (or ground beat), moving at a certain rate (the tempo), into groupings which are a stated number of beats (the bar) and which include strong and weak beats in an organized pattern. All this is implied by a "meter" of 4/4, 3/4, and so on.

Modal: (1) Said of a section, or a whole tune, having static harmony (using one chord) and using scales from a particular mode, most typically the Dorian; (2) having a key feeling derived not from dynamic chord progressions (like circle of fifths) but rather from repetition.

Modern: The styles of jazz since 1945. Especially applied to bebop, cool jazz, and hard bop.

Modulation: The establishment of a new key. This is mainly a matter of harmonic progression, but expectation, emphasis, and phrasing also enter into determining whether a new key has really been established. In standards, a modulation to the beginning of the bridge is strongly expected. Typically, a II-V or a iii-VI-ii-V progression in the new key is used.

Montuno: A term of Latin music in jazz. (1) An indefinitely repeated pattern of one, two, or four bars in the piano, typically with ingeniously syncopated moving inner voices and a differently syncopated bass line; (2) incorrectly, a pyramiding vamp in which one instrument enters alone, then another is added.

Moving inner voice: A prominent line played by a voice in between the melody and the bass.

Neo-bop: The new bebop style of several successful players in the 1990s.

Open voicing: One in which the chord tones are spread out over a greater range.

Original: A tune composed by a jazz musician and played by them but perhaps not well known to others.

Out: The last chorus of a tune, when the head is played for the last time.

Outer voice: The melody line or the bass, the top or bottom line.

Outro: The opposite of intro, it is an added ending section.

Outside: A way of playing over changes that avoids using the normal scales or has no relationship to the changes. Commonly used in "free jazz" playing nonharmonic tones.

Pattern: A preplanned melodic figure, repeated at different pitch levels. Something played automatically by the fingers without much thought. See "Riff."

Pedal: A bass line that stays mainly on one note (or its octaves) under several changes of harmony. Also known as pedal-point.

Pentatonic: Pertaining to scales of five notes to the octave, in particular, 1-2-3-5-6 of the major scale. Pentatonic melodies are typical of much indigenous music around the world, and these scales are also an important part of the modern jazz sound. Pentatonic melodies and patterns were especially typical of jazz and fusion in the 1970s. Playing the black piano keys as a scale. It can be major or minor.

Pickup: A phrase beginning that comes before the beginning of the first bar. A pickup can be one note or a longer phrase. Known in classical music as an anacrusis.

Pocket: "In the pocket" means perfectly in time, especially bass playing that is "in the center" of the beat (rather than slightly leading or dragging the beat). Used in fusion and funk and is often called a "groove."

Polytonality: The use of two different keys simultaneously. True polytonality is rare.
Progression: A definite series of chords, forming a passage with some harmonic unity or dramatic meaning. Commonly known as changes.
Quality: The character of a chord given by its third, fifth, and seventh. The qualities are major, dominant, minor, tonic minor, half-diminished, and diminished. In theory, augmented major and augmented (dominant) would also be qualities, but they are usually just considered alterations.
Quartal: Based on fourths. Chords built up of fourths were, famously, developed by pianist McCoy Tyner.
Quote: A short piece of some other well-known tune thrown into a solo. A good quote is unexpected, incongruous, and yet seems to fit perfectly. Some quotes are clichés.
Remote key: A key distant on the circle of fifths from the original one, such as E major compared to C major.
Rhythm changes: The chords to "I Got Rhythm" (Gershwin), somewhat modified and simplified. Many jazz tunes use these changes, and every player must know them. There are several variations.
Rhythm section: The piano, bass, and drums in a combo, those who play throughout the tune, behind the soloists. Can also include guitar or vibes, or there might be no piano.
Riff: A relatively simple, catchy repeated phrase. May be played behind a soloist or as part of a head. Sometimes it is a quote or cliché in short form.
Root: The fundamental pitch on which a chord is based, from which the chord takes its name, and to which the other tones of the chord are a third, fifth or seventh above.
Scales: (1) A selection of tones in the octave, arranged in ascending or descending order, usually but not always using intervals of half- or whole-steps, and using the same notes in every successive octave. One tone is usually thought of as being the root, but it need not be the first note played. Most scales have five, six, seven, or eight notes to the octave. (2) Modes in jazz are considered scales and include whole-tone forms, blues scales, and pentatonic and chromatic forms.

Shed: Short for "woodshed"—to practice.

Shell: A two-note structure in the left hand consisting of the root and one other note, usually the seventh, the third or tenth, or the sixth.

Shout chorus: A special, complete, through-composed chorus played just before the final out-chorus. Used to close out a big band composition or arrangement, a punctuation for a piece.

Sideman: Any member of a band or small group other than the leader.

Solo: Any one player's improvisation over one or more choruses of the tune (occasionally, especially in ballads, less than one chorus). A distinction is made between soloing and playing the head.

Song form: A musical form with two contrasting themes A and B, thus A (eight bars); A repeated; B (eight bars); A repeated. The three As have slightly different endings (turnarounds). Another common form may be called song form also: ABAB (the second B starting like the first but ending differently). Most older standards are in song form.

Stand: The bandstand or stage.

Standard: A tune universally accepted and played by many jazz musicians. Many standards are Broadway songs from the 1930s, 1940s, and 1950s. Others are strictly jazz compositions that have been accepted by a large number of jazz artists.

Straight eighths: With equal, even eighth notes. Same as "Latin."

Stride: The typical piano style of the 1930s, tending toward virtuosity. The left hand plays alternating low-register bass notes (or octaves, fifths or tenths) and middle register rootless voicings, giving an "oom-pah" effect, interspersed with stepwise parallel tenths. The right hand often employs busy runs, arpeggios, and octaves or full chords. Suggestions of stride remain in the technique of many of today's players.

Stroll: A style led by the bass, played at a relaxed pace.

Substitution: A chord put in the place of a different chord. A substitution can be made throughout a tune or just improvised at a particular moment. Usually the idea is that the root of the chord is changed, while the other voices are common to both chords.

Swing: (1) The style of the 1930s, when the big band was the dominant form of jazz; (2) a rhythmic manner, unique to jazz, in which the first of a pair of written eighth notes is played longer than the second, even twice as long, while the second tends to receive a slight accent, though the distribution of accents is irregular and syncopated. The syllables doo-bay are used to show the long-short relationship. The degree of this effect depends on the overall tempo and is modified by the requirements of expression and phrasing. (3) As a direction in a chart, played with a swing feel, as opposed to Latin. Jazz players are expected to "feel" the undefined feel.

Syncopation: Accents placed on the offbeat or weak portions of a beat. In 4/4 time accents are on beats two and four and/or on the second eighth note in a group of eighth notes or eighth note that follows an eighth note rest.

Technique: The ability of instrumental and vocal musicians to exert optimal control of their instruments or vocal cords in order to produce the precise musical effects they desire.

Tenor: Refers to the tenor saxophone known as the "jazz tenor."

Tetrachord: A four-note portion of a scale. For example, the diminished scale is composed of two tetrachords with identical interval constructions.

Timbre: Tone quality, characteristic instrumental sound.

Time feel: (1) The subjective impression of which time unit constitutes one beat and how long a bar is; (2) the emotional quality of the rhythm.

Tonic minor: A scale/chord with a minor third and a major sixth and seventh, generally used for the tonic or home chord in minor keys. Distinguished from other minor chord functions.

Top: The beginning point of each chorus, the first beat of the first measure.

Trading fours (or eights, twos): A form of discontinuous drum solo in which four-measure sections are alternately played solo by the drummer and by another soloist (who goes first). The latter can be one particular soloist throughout, or it can cycle through the different instruments. Also, two different instrumental soloists can trade fours with each other, such as the trumpet and the sax. This is called a chase. Trading fours usually goes on for one or two choruses.

Transpose: To write or perform (a composition) in a key other than the original or given key, most often to accommodate the range of a vocalist or another instrument. To write notes for instruments that are not based on C.

Triad: Concretely, a chord of three notes—the root, third, and fifth—played together in close position in one of the three inversions.

Tritone: The interval of three whole-steps, that is, an augmented fourth or diminished fifth.

Tritone substitution: The substitution of a chord whose root is a tritone away. See "Substitution."

Tune: A single jazz composition or jazz performance, a piece. The word "song" is generally not used by jazz musicians.

Turnaround: A sequence of chords, or the portion of a tune that they occupy, that forms a cadence at the end of a section of a tune, definitively establishes the tonic key, and leads back to the opening chord of the next section, or to the top. Typically the turnaround chords are ii-V-I or iii-vi-ii-V-I for one or two measures preceding the return to the top (measure 1).

Up: In a fast tempo.

Vamp: A simple section, like a riff, designed to be repeated as often as necessary, especially one at the beginning of a tune. Generally four or eight bars. Also a constantly repeated bass line over which a solo is played.

Verse: In many older standard songs, an introductory section, often rubato, that leads up to the "chorus" or main strain.

Voice: Any one of the melodic lines formed by the flow of the music. The bass line and the melody form the two outer voices, and the tones in between may, to a greater or lesser extent, form melodic lines of their own, called inner voices.

Voice-leading: The succession of harmonic tones in the inner voices to form coherent melodic lines of their own, or, at least, to move in a smooth, mainly step-wise motion.

Voicing: A particular arrangement of the notes of a chord in which chosen harmonies color the tone.

Walk: In bass playing, to play mostly one note per beat, making a smooth, continuous quarter-note line. The pianist can also walk with their left hand.

Whole-tone: A six-note scale, of which there are two, made up entirely of whole-step intervals, or the harmonies derived from it.

X: Time. Thus "4X" on a chart means "[play] four times."

Index

accuracy, stylistic, 36
accurate cross listening, 38
accurate jazz interpretation, 36
acoustic/electric bass, 14
activities and programs, 106
activity coordinator, 103
Adderley, Cannonball, 42
adjudication, 55–58
adjudication form, 115
adjudicators, 56, 59, 61, 107
adjudicators form, 110
Aebersold, Jamey, 22, 25, 41, 79
Aebersold jazz voicings, 22
Aeolian, 40
Air Force's Airmen, 17
air travel, 111; international, 112
Alfred Music Publishing, 87
Alto Sax, 26
Amazing Slow Downer, 20, 83
Appendix, 121–22
arpeggios, 13, 43, 45–46
articulation markings, 108
articulations, stylistic, 36
ASCAP, 77

assessments, 7, 55–56, 66, 107–8
assessments and festivals, 107
attacks, 37–38, 49–51, 74, 116; clean, 49; hard, 38
attire purchases/maintenance, special, 105
audio, 21, 52, 117
audio systems, 64–65
audition material, 15
awards and recognition, 72, 104

balance of chords, 28
band and orchestra classroom, 78
band boosters group, 101, 104
band budget, 63, 65, 67
band director and jazz director groups, 66
band director teaching jazz, 80
band handbook, 15
Band-in-a-Box, 20
bank of scales and patterns, 40
Barnhouse, 87
bars/measures, 16
bass amplifier, 64

bass player, 23, 25
beats, strong, 21, 23
bebop, 60
best microphone setup, 117
best model rhythm sections, 22
best notation software, 81
best recording console, 76
big band charts, 28–29
big band pieces, 28
big bands, 17, 25, 27–29
big band setup, 27
big band solos, 27
block chords, 16, 29
Blue Bossa, 38
blues, basic, 22
blues form, 16
blues scales, 34–36, 39–40
blues songs, 16
blues standards, 79
BMI, 77
books for improvisation, 79
books for music educators, 139
booster group bylaws, 104
Brandt, Carl, 22
brass instruments, 26, 29
brass players, 54
brass section, 26
budget, 8, 63–68, 75, 81–82; maintenance, 8; operating, 65
budget development, 102
buses, securing, 14, 71, 111
business manager, 64, 102–3

cables, 67–68
CDs, 22, 68, 79
challenges learning jazz, 2
chaperone requirements, 112
choosing literature, 87, 89
chord changes, 35
chord choices, 25
chord forms, 22

chord progressions, 11, 23, 29, 37, 41, 45
chords: dominant seventh, 16; major seventh, 16; minor-minor, 16
chord spellings, common, 22
chord symbols, 23
Clarke, Kenny, 24
class description, 15
Coker, Jerry, 25
Coltrane, John, 42, 46
common setups for microphones, 117
comping, 25
composers, 11, 77, 79, 87
compositions, spontaneous, 11, 41
conductor, 23, 27, 33, 76, 110
Conn-Selmer, 80
Count Basie Orchestra, 17, 22
countermelodies, 26

Davis, Miles, 125–26
Decca Tree setup, 76
developing a five-year plan, 8, 69
developing improvisational skills, 39, 41, 43, 45, 47
devices, handheld, 68, 76–77, 84
diminuendo/decrescendo, 59
directors, 16, 23, 44, 51, 56, 60, 64, 103–5
Dixieland, 60
doo-bay, 42
Dorian, 40
drum set, 8, 14, 24, 67, 117
drum set equipment, 71
dynamics, 31, 59, 82

ear development, 42
electric bass, 64, 98, 117
electric keyboard, 64

electronic instruments and maintenance and repairs of electronic equipment, 63
electronic tuners, 67
Ellington, Duke, 37
ensemble balance, 28
equipment replacement/ purchases, 65
expenses, 65–66, 78

festival information and description, 55
festival preparation, 55, 57, 59, 61
finale, 81, 83
first rehearsal and classroom management, 32
first rehearsal piece, 33, 37
focus on teaching skills, 32
forming committees, 105
fundraising, 6–7, 101–2, 104, 109

general handbook description, 6
Google, 81, 84
Green, Freddie, 22, 25
guided listening, 19, 35, 108, 115
guided listening exercises, 34, 61, 68
guitar amplifier, 64
guitar and bass, 32

Haerle, 22, 25
handbook, 5–7, 9, 56, 66, 105
Harry Fox Agency, 77
head, 20, 35
Hefti, Neal, 37
HFA Songfile, 77
high-definition video recording, 84

improvisation, 11, 13, 20, 41, 45, 48, 72, 74, 79

improvisers, 13–14, 25, 40–41, 43–47
instrumentation, unbalanced, 15
instrument maintenance, 91, 93, 95, 97, 99
intonation, 27, 32–33, 36–37, 49–50, 74, 116
Ionian, 40
iReal Pro, 20, 83

Jamey Aebersold Play-A-Long, 79
Jammates, 20, 83
jazz, 3–4, 9, 11–12, 16, 19–22, 42, 49, 52–53, 72, 79, 104
Jazz Boosters Organization, 104
jazz charts, 25
jazz ensembles, 1, 5, 14–15, 21, 23, 27–29, 33, 49–50, 64, 66–67, 87–89, 101, 103–6, 108, 121–22
jazz group to swing, 23
jazz interpretation, 50
jazz musicians, 39
jazz program, 1, 5, 8, 63, 101–3
jazz/rock pieces, 37–38
jazz/rock voicings, 22
Johnston, Cynthia, 85
Jones, Jo, 22, 24
JW Pepper and SheetMusicPlus, 87

Kenton, Stan, 17
knowledge, chord/scale, 39

Lateef, Yusef, 40
Latin pieces, 37, 79
Leadership Function, 103
learning jazz styles, 15
lesson plans, 4, 16, 36, 50–51, 57, 81

listening, 13–14, 19, 21, 40–41, 43, 61, 71, 74–75, 84, 108, 116
listening skills, 39
Lydian, 40, 128–29

matching pair of microphones, 117
McBride, Christian 17
melody, 20, 26, 32, 35, 41, 45, 59
microphone placement, 116, 118
microphones in front, 75, 116–17
Mixolydian, 40–41
Music Booster Manual, 101

National Association for Music Education (NAfME), 4, 7, 85, 101
National Standards, 4
Navy Commodores, 17

Page, Walter, 22–23
patterns, 20, 24–25, 40, 42, 44, 46, 117
Permission Slip, 121–22
philosophy, 4, 69
piano, 14–15, 22, 25, 29, 46, 117
plan, five-year, 8, 69–70, 72
playing block chords, 29
Powell, Bud, 124
practice jazz melodies, 79
preparing program notes, 77
program development, 11, 64, 69

quick repairs and instrument maintenance, 91, 93, 95, 97, 99

recording tips, 76, 85, 119
repairs, emergency, 91, 94–95
rhythm changes, 37

rhythm section, 12, 21–23, 27, 39, 51–52, 61, 117
ride cymbal, 24
Roemer, Clinton, 22

sample first rehearsal, 34
sample jazz ensemble handbook, 5
sample lesson plan, 36
Satin Doll, 51
saxophone section, 26–27
scales and arpeggios, 46
selecting students, 14
shout chorus, 132
Sibelius, 81, 83
skills: cross-listening, 31, 34; developing language, 43; sight-reading, 78
Smartmusic, 78–79, 82–83
software, 20, 67, 82–83
solos, transcribed, 42, 79
Sonnymoon for two, 34, 36
spang-a-lang, 24
spontaneously composing, 40
style, 13, 15, 19, 21–22, 24–25, 28, 33, 37, 58, 60
style accuracy, 56
suggested arrangers, 89
suggested composers, 88
suggested publishers, 87

tablets and smartphones, 77, 83
teaching improvisation, 14, 39
teaching jazz concepts, 16
techniques, 14, 51
tone quality, 50, 61
transcribing jazz solos, 42
travel expenses, 65–66
trips and festivals, 107, 109, 111, 113

trombones, 15, 27, 29, 33, 97
trumpets, 26–29, 95–97

uniform/wardrobe
  maintenance/purchase, 103
unit plans, 34, 36, 69
US copyright laws, 77

voices, 29

Warner Bros., 22
Weiskopf, Walt, 40
writing lesson plans for jazz
  class, 50

X/Y setup, 76

Zoom, 21, 76, 80, 84

About the Author

Ronald E. Kearns is a retired band, orchestra, and jazz band director. He is a classically trained musician, jazz recording artist, and jazz record producer with over forty-five commercially produced recordings, the author of three books for music educators, an international music adjudicator, a Vandoren of Paris Performing Artist and Clinician, a Selmer of Paris Performing Artist and Clinician, and a private saxophone and flute instructor. This book is part 3 of his Quick Reference for Band Directors series. Ron's other books for music educators are *Quick Reference for Band Directors* (Rowman and Littlefield), *Recording Tips for Music Educators* (Oxford University Press), and *Quick Reference for Band Directors Who Teach Orchestra* (Rowman and Littlefield). Ron's jazz ensembles never received less than Superior ratings at national and international festivals and assessments. He has published many articles on jazz for *WAVE Magazine* and Vandoren of Paris. Those articles have been widely accepted by band directors and music educators and are sources for this book.

www.ingramcontent.com/pod-product-compliance
Lightning Source LLC
Chambersburg PA
CBHW030556230426
43661CB00054B/2158